To the R
From GRANDMA & GRANDPA

CHRISTMAS 2007

# The Usborne
# Big Book of
# Things to Spot

Illustrated by Teri Gower

Written by Ruth Brocklehurst,
Gillian Doherty and Anna Milbourne

Designed by Susannah Owen

# Contents

# 1001
## Animals to Spot

# Contents

# Animals to spot

The pictures in this section show animals living all around the world. In each picture there are lots of different kinds of animals for you to find and count. The example pages below show what you need to do to find them all.

This amazing underwater scene is on pages 18–19.

Each little picture shows you what to look for in the big picture.

The blue number tells you how many of that animal you need to spot.

In the ocean

8 cuttlefish

9 seahorses

10 barracudas

10 clown fish  3 sharks  8 shrimps  3 manta rays  10 snappers  6 dolphins  7 parrot fish

This is Leo the artist. He draws animals everywhere he goes. Can you spot his drawing pad in the scenes in this section?

On pages 34 and 35 there are two more puzzles for you to do.

# On the farm

3 puppies　　5 ducks　　9 ducklings　　8 black lambs　　10 black and white lambs

6 hens

4 brown foals

10 chicks

6 cows

10 calves

# On safari

10 ostriches    4 hippos    5 lion cubs    4 elephants    6 giraffes

6 rhinos

 10 zebras

 8 vultures

 9 warthogs

 10 gazelles

# In the desert

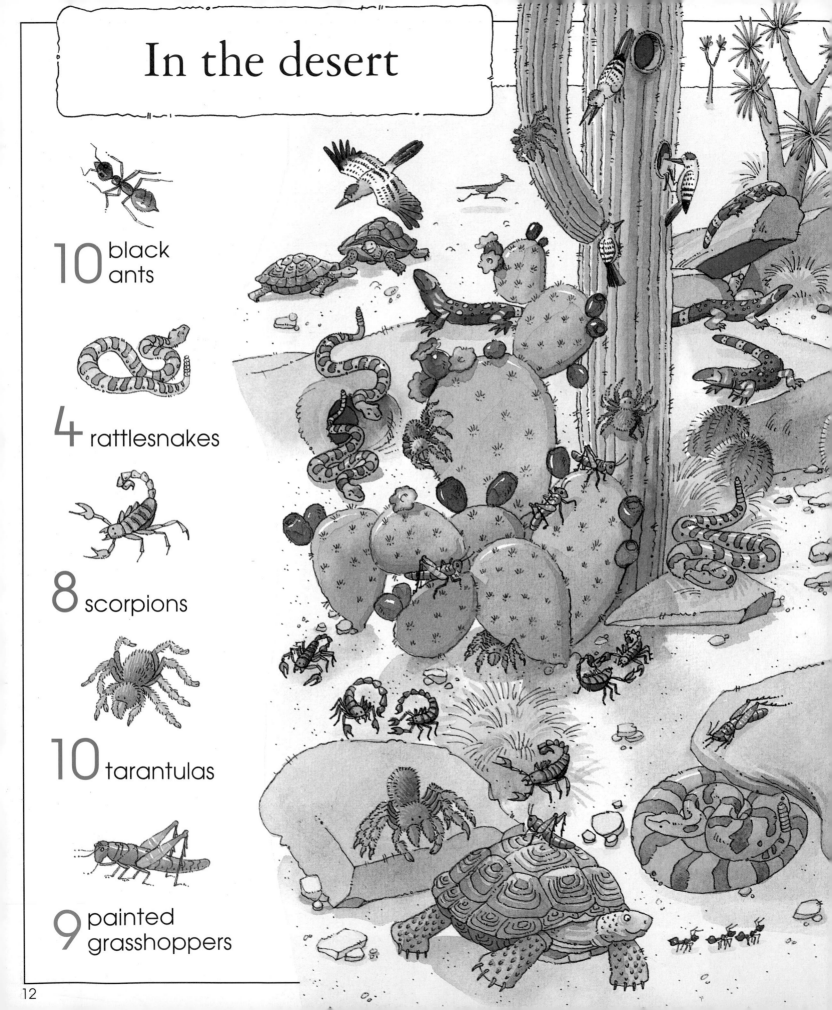

10 black ants

4 rattlesnakes

8 scorpions

10 tarantulas

9 painted grasshoppers

6 woodpeckers

4 jack rabbits

5 tortoises

7 gila monsters

3 coyotes

# In the Arctic

10 caribou

4 polar bears

 10 seals

 6 snowy owls

 9 lemmings

 1 humpback whale

 6 Arctic foxes

 4 killer whales

 8 baby seals

5 narwhals

15

# In the woods

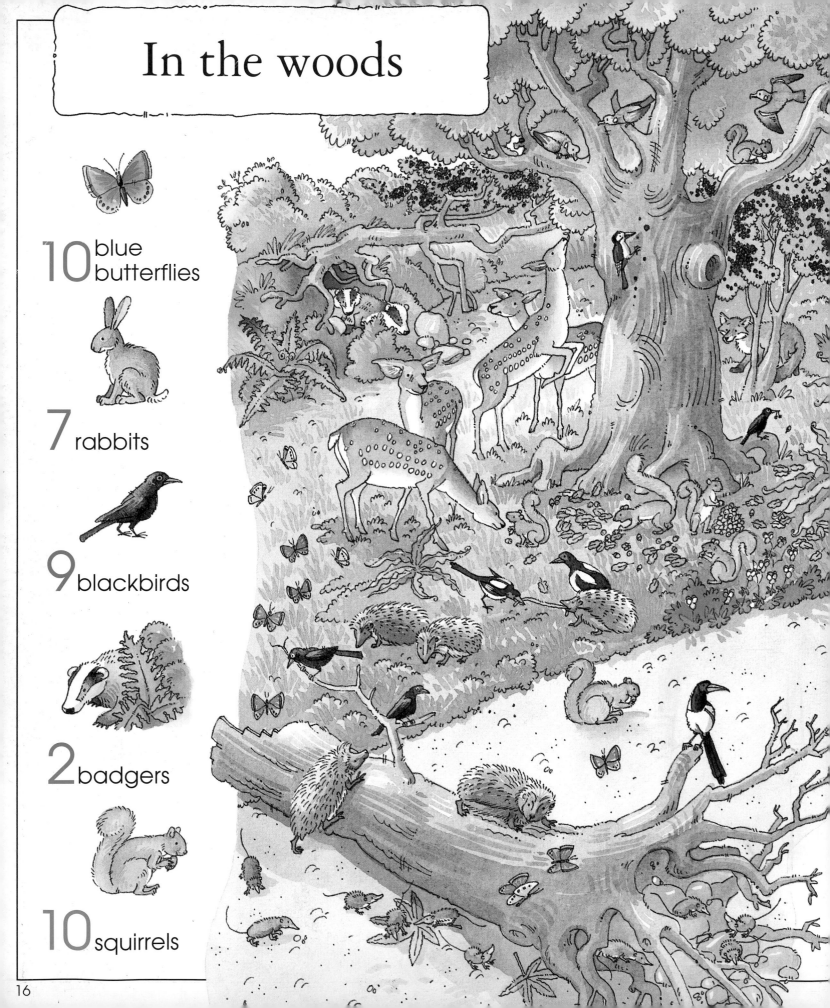

**10** blue butterflies

**7** rabbits

**9** blackbirds

**2** badgers

**10** squirrels

16

8 wood pigeons   7 deer   10 hedgehogs   5 foxes   10 shrews

# In the ocean

10 clown fish  3 sharks

8 cuttlefish

9 seahorses

10 barracudas

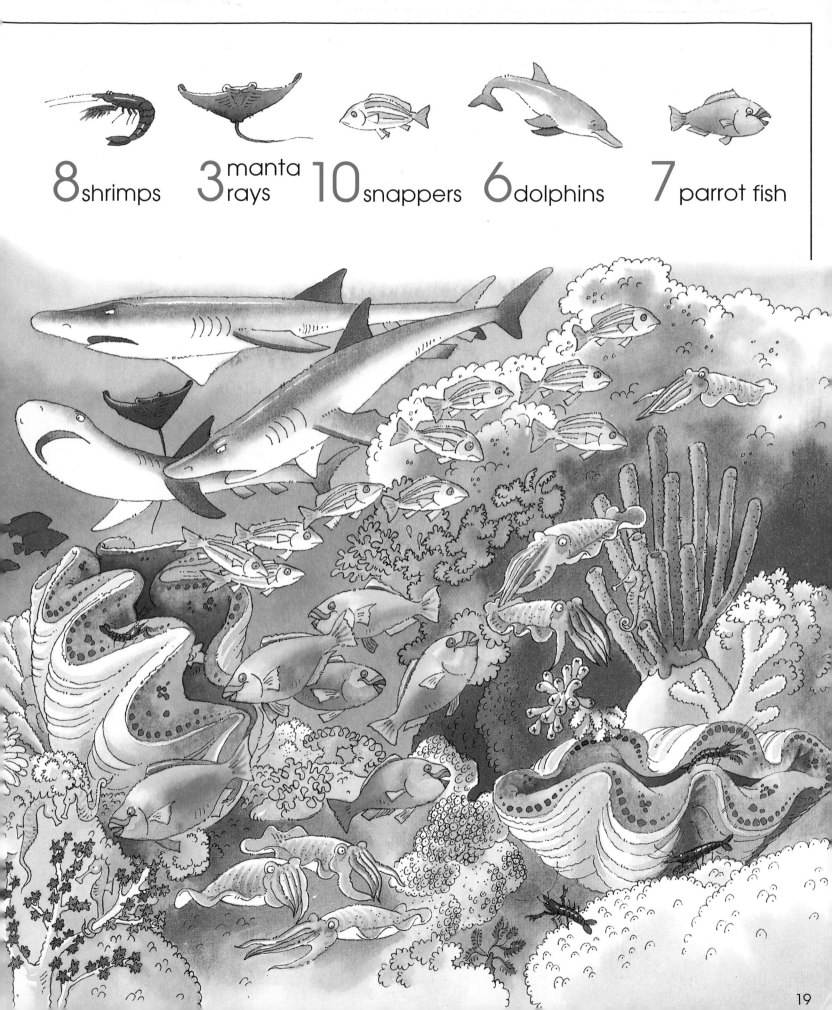

8 shrimps    3 manta rays    10 snappers    6 dolphins    7 parrot fish

# In the rainforest

5 sloths

7 arrow-poison frogs

8 toucans

3 coral snakes

1 jaguar

9 parrots

7 spider monkeys

10 egrets

5 armadillos

8 boas

# In the garden

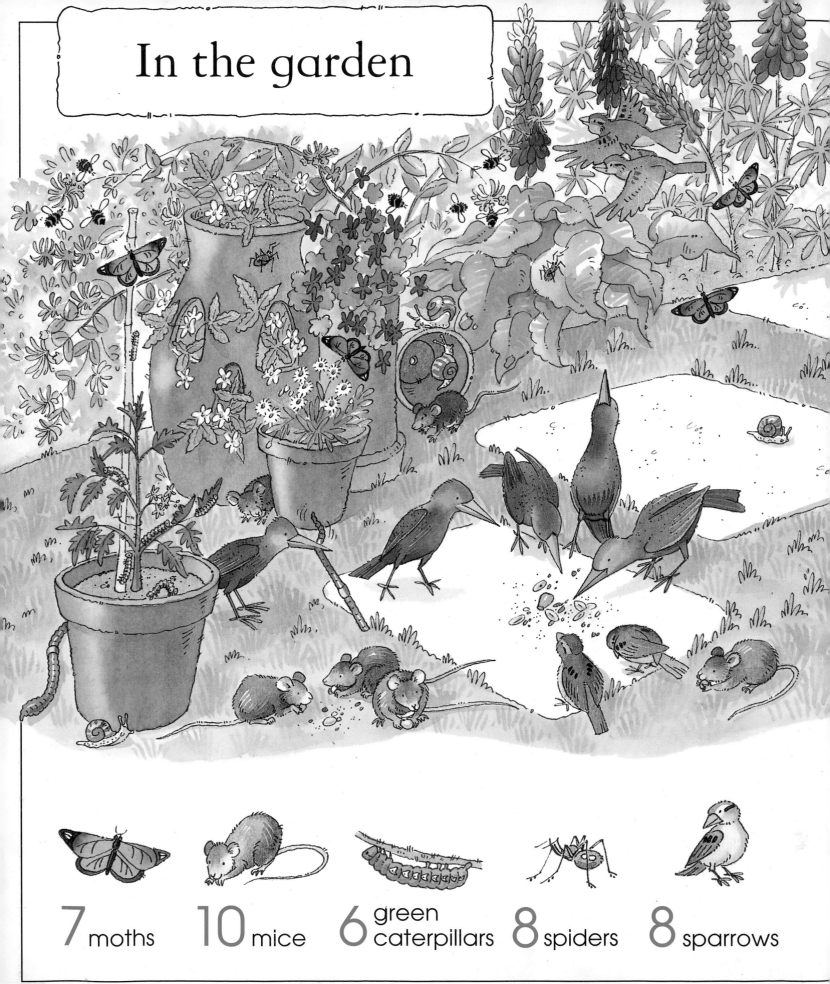

7 moths   10 mice   6 green caterpillars   8 spiders   8 sparrows

10 bees    9 snails    2 kittens    8 starlings    6 worms

# In the outback

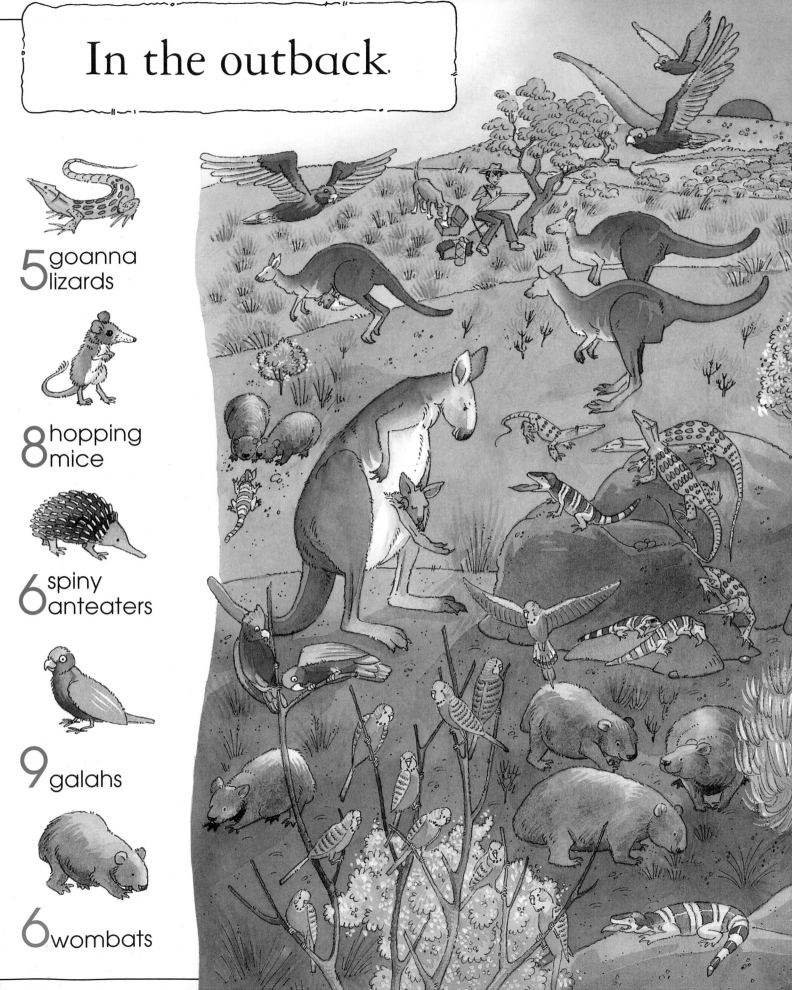

5 goanna lizards

8 hopping mice

6 spiny anteaters

9 galahs

6 wombats

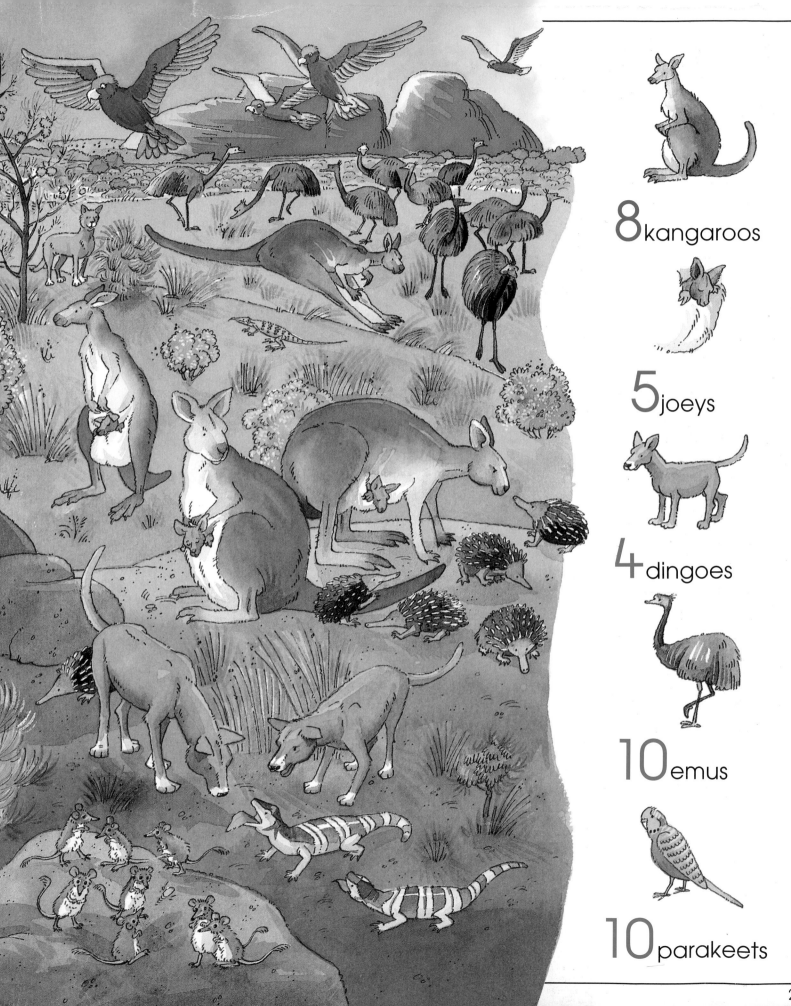

8 kangaroos

5 joeys

4 dingoes

10 emus

10 parakeets

# In the swamp

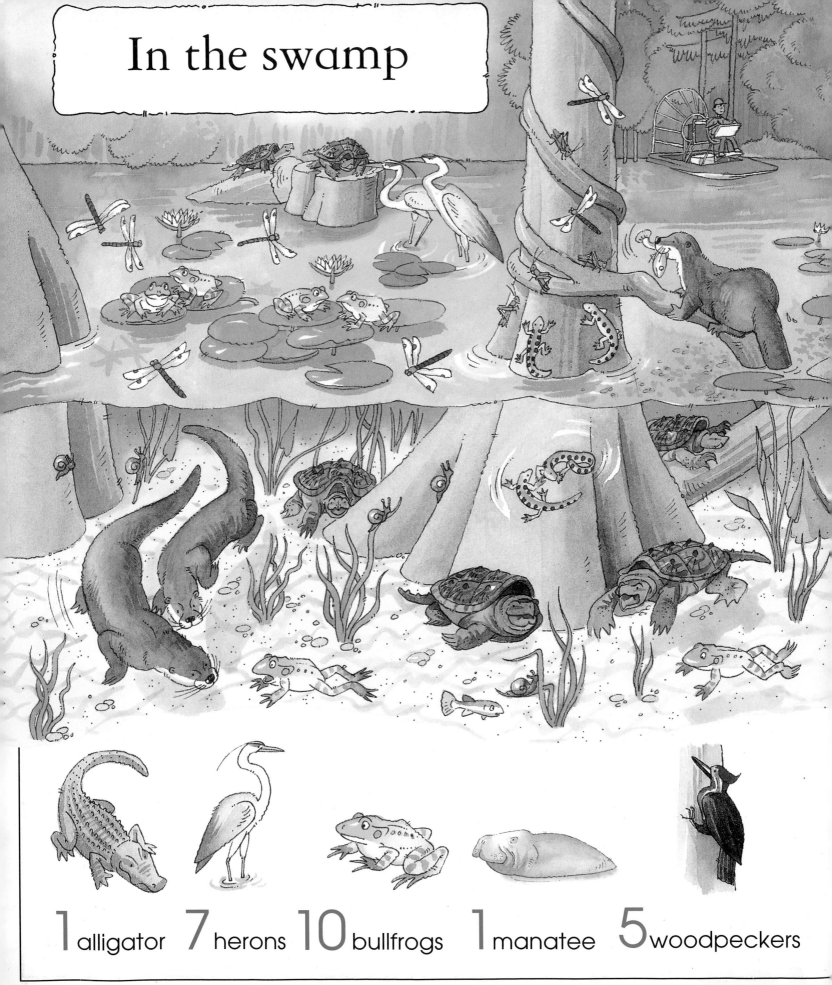

1 alligator  7 herons  10 bullfrogs  1 manatee  5 woodpeckers

8 newts  10 apple snails 10 dragonflies  9 turtles  9 grasshoppers

# In the mountains

10 butterflies

9 pikas

9 mountain goats

5 eagles

10 geese 7 marmots 3 vultures 1 snow leopard 3 black bears

5 yaks

# By the sea

5 oystercatchers

10 mussels

6 crabs

8 seagulls

6 sea urchins

6 seals

5 squat lobsters

10 winkles

10 limpets

7 sea anemones

# Children's farm

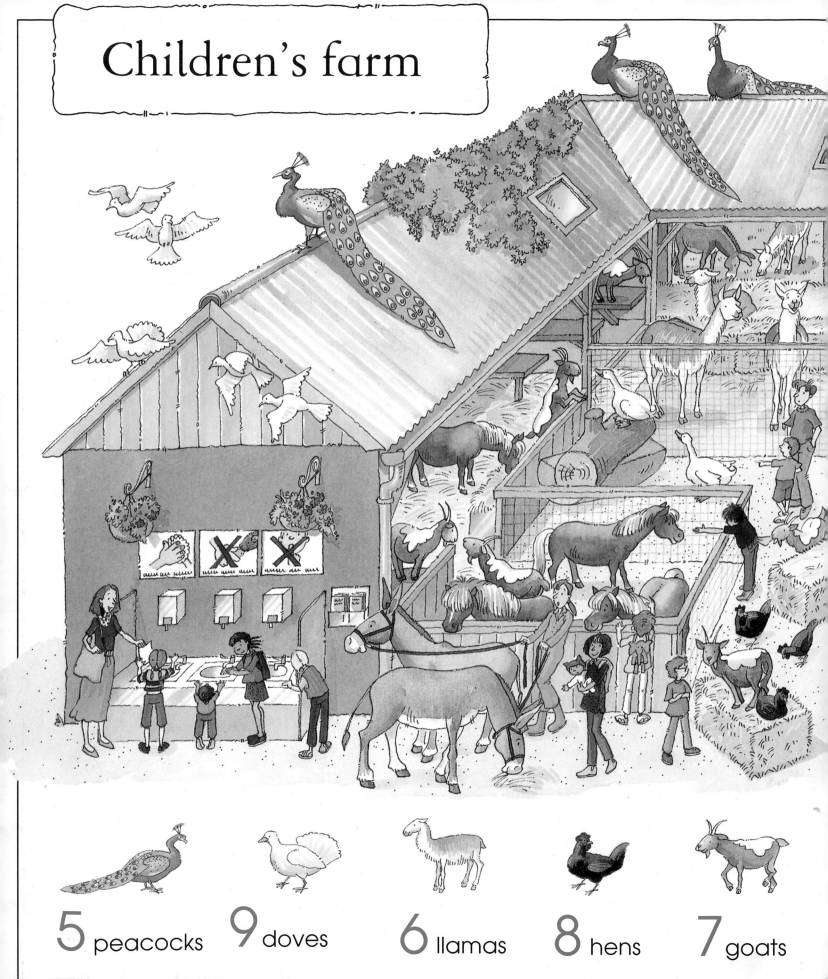

**5** peacocks   **9** doves   **6** llamas   **8** hens   **7** goats

**10** ducks

**5** Shetland ponies

**10** guinea pigs

**3** camels

**10** rabbits

# Leo's pictures

Here are some pictures of animals that Leo drew on his travels. Look back through this section and see if you can find and count them all.

6 otters

9 scarlet ibises

5 magpies

10 wildebeests

7 blue-tongued skinks

9 puffins

10 hairy caterpillars

3 giant clams

9 red ants

10 wallcreepers

4 turkeys

10 walruses

# Close-ups

Inside each of these circles there is a close-up view of an animal from one of the scenes earlier in this section. Using the clues, can you name each animal?

Whose stripes are these?

Which animal has just one long tusk?

Who has a blue tongue like this?

Which animal looks like a striped horse?

Whose powerful antlers are these?

Whose tail feathers look like eyes?

Which bird has bright feathers like these?

Whose trumpeting trunk is this?

Which orange striped fish has a funny name?

Which hopping insect has legs like these?

Which fish has green and yellow stripes?

Which animal has a very long neck?

# Answers

Did you manage to find all the animals from Leo's pictures and recognize the animals from the close-up pictures? Here's where they are.

## Leo's pictures

**6 otters**
In the swamp
(pages 26 and 27)

**9 scarlet ibises**
In the rainforest
(pages 20 and 21)

**5 magpies**
In the woods
(pages 16 and 17)

**10 wildebeests**
On safari
(pages 10 and 11)

**7 blue-tongued skinks**
In the outback
(pages 24 and 25)

**9 puffins**
By the sea
(pages 30 and 31)

**10 hairy caterpillars**
In the garden
(pages 22 and 23)

**3 giant clams**
In the ocean
(pages 18 and 19)

**9 red ants**
In the desert
(pages 12 and 13)

**10 wallcreepers**
In the mountains
(pages 28 and 29)

**4 turkeys**
On the farm
(pages 8 and 9)

**10 walruses**
In the Arctic
(pages 14 and 15)

## Close-ups

coral snake
(pages 20 and 21)

narwhal
(pages 14 and 15)

blue-tongued skink
(pages 24 and 25)

zebra
(pages 10 and 11)

caribou
(pages 14 and 15)

peacock
(pages 32 and 33)

parrot
(pages 20 and 21)

elephant
(pages 10 and 11)

clown fish
(pages 18 and 19)

painted grasshopper
(pages 12 and 13)

snapper
(pages 18 and 19)

giraffe
(pages 10 and 11)

**Acknowledgements**

Natural history consultant:
Dr. Margaret Rostron
Editor: Anna Milbourne
Managing editor: Felicity Brooks
Managing designer: Mary Cartwright
Additional design: Doriana Berkovic

Digital manipulation: John Russell

The publishers would also like to thank the staff at London Zoo's Children's Zoo for their help in the preparation of pages 32 and 33.

# 1001

## Things to Spot
## on the Farm

# Contents

# Things to spot

The pictures in this section show different kinds of farms. You can peer inside a henhouse, see cowboys rounding up cows on a ranch and find out what happens on a rice farm. On every page there are lots of things for you to find and count.

This milking scene is on pages 46–47.

There's a red balloon hidden in each big picture.

Each little picture shows you what to look for in the big picture.

The blue number shows how many of that thing you need to find.

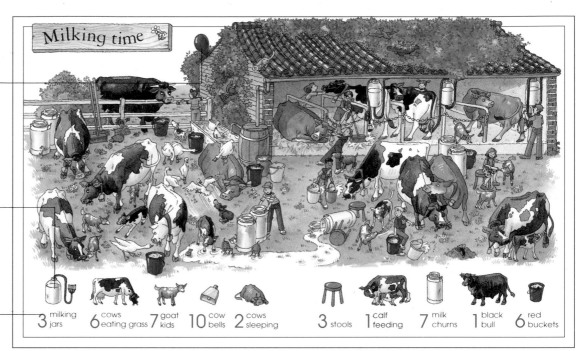

Milking time

3 milking jars

6 cows eating grass

7 goat kids

10 cow bells

2 cows sleeping

3 stools

1 calf feeding

7 milk churns

1 black bull

6 red buckets

Can you find everything you need to make a scarecrow like this one? Find out what you need to look for on page 66. There's an extra page of puzzles on page 67 too.

39

# The sheep farm

10 white sheep with black faces    3 dogs    1 shearing machine    8 lambs    10 poppies

9 rabbits

2 pairs of clippers

4 sheep with horns

3 shepherds' crooks

5 black sheep

# The fruit farm

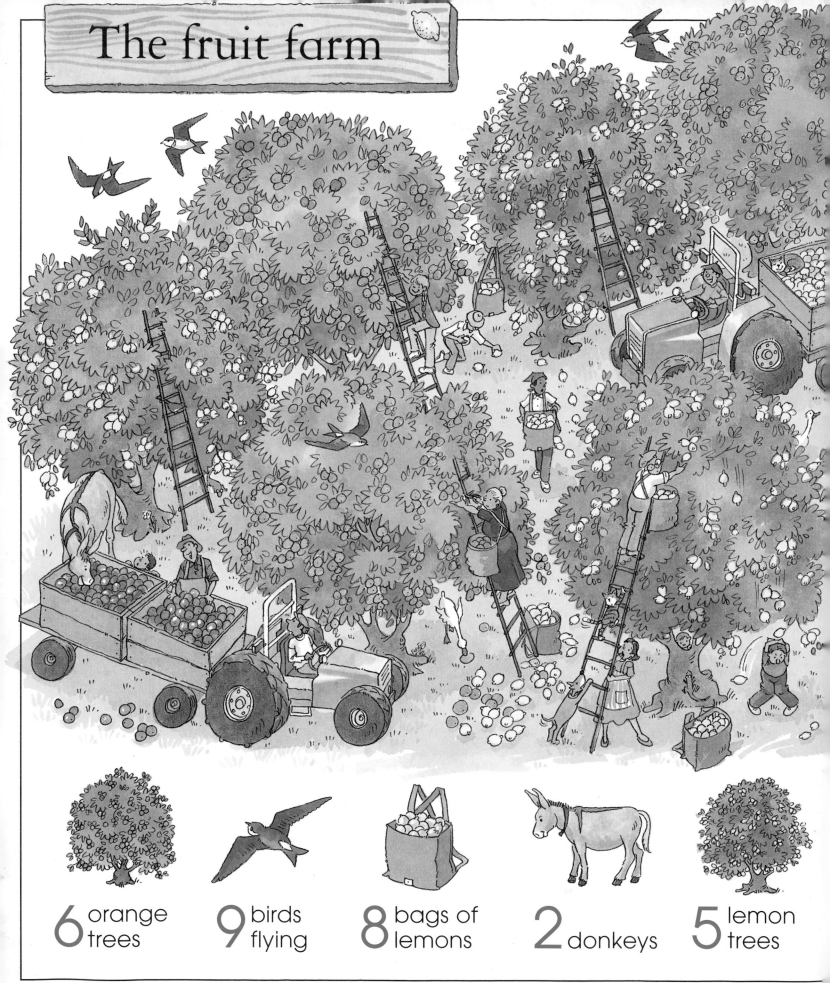

**6** orange trees

**9** birds flying

**8** bags of lemons

**2** donkeys

**5** lemon trees

10 lizards   7 baskets of grapes   2 tractors   7 ladders   3 striped cats

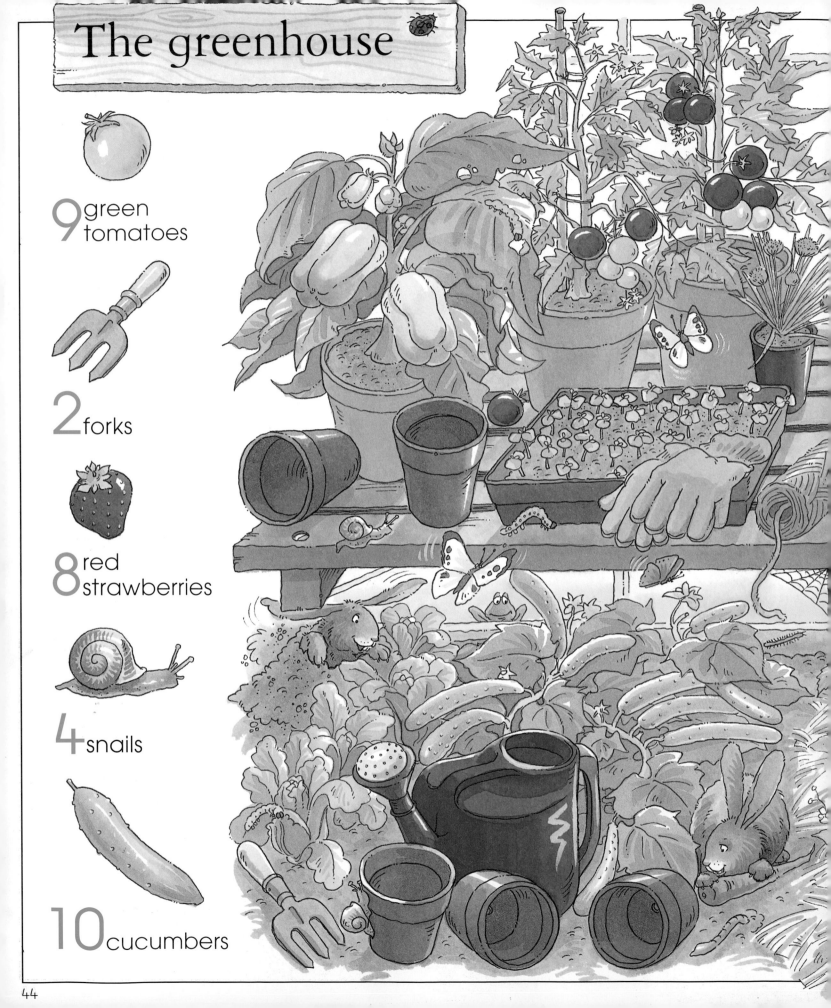

# The greenhouse

9 green tomatoes

2 forks

8 red strawberries

4 snails

10 cucumbers

10 red tomatoes

2 watering cans

5 caterpillars

7 empty plant pots

2 seed trays

45

# Milking time

 **3** milking jars

 **6** cows eating grass

 **7** goat kids

 **10** cow bells

**2** cows sleeping

**3** stools

 **1** calf feeding

 **7** milk churns

 **1** black bull

 **6** red buckets

# Baby animals

10 chicks

1 calf

7 lambs

5 puppies

2 foals

48

7 clean pink piglets

6 striped kittens

3 muddy piglets

4 black kittens

2 goat kids

# Harvest time

**1** combine harvester    **10** seagulls    **1** blue tractor    **9** rabbits    **10** bales of straw

1 baling machine    9 crows    2 grain trailers    3 red tractors    4 foxes

# At the stables

7 saddles

6 bales of hay

5 sponges

2 foals

1 horse trailer

52

10 riding hats  3 black horses  7 forks  3 horse blankets  6 brown hens

# The henhouse

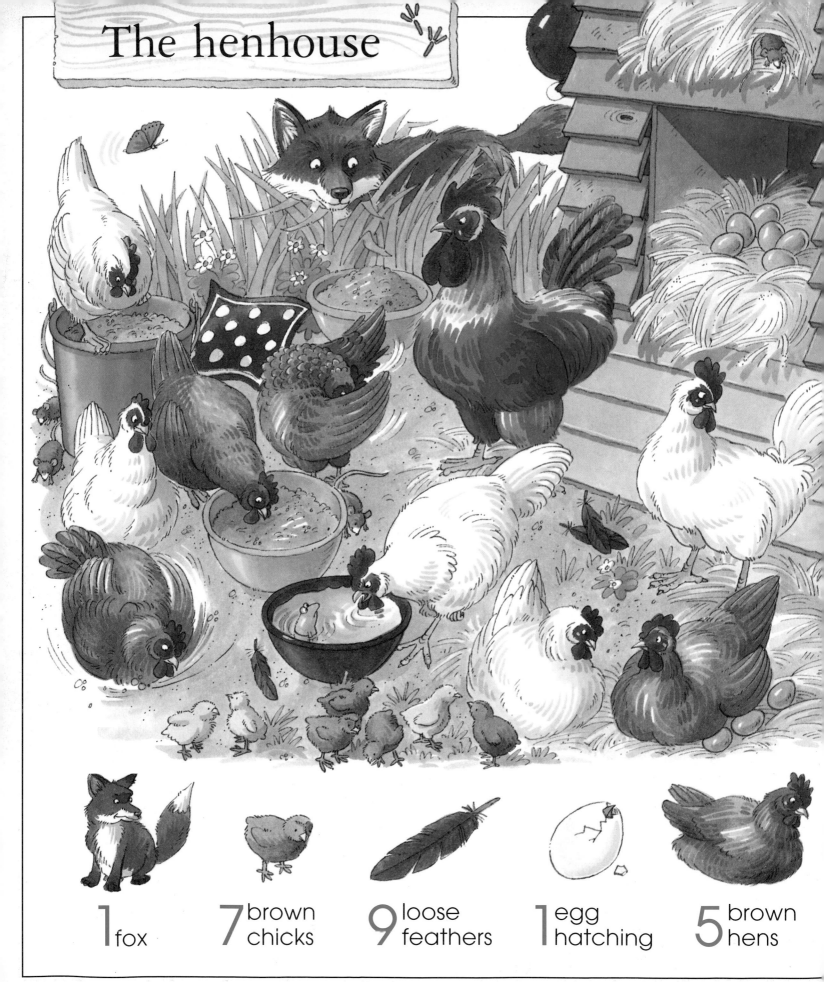

1 fox

7 brown chicks

9 loose feathers

1 egg hatching

5 brown hens

8 mice    10 yellow chicks    2 bowls of grain    10 brown eggs    9 white hens

# The rice fields

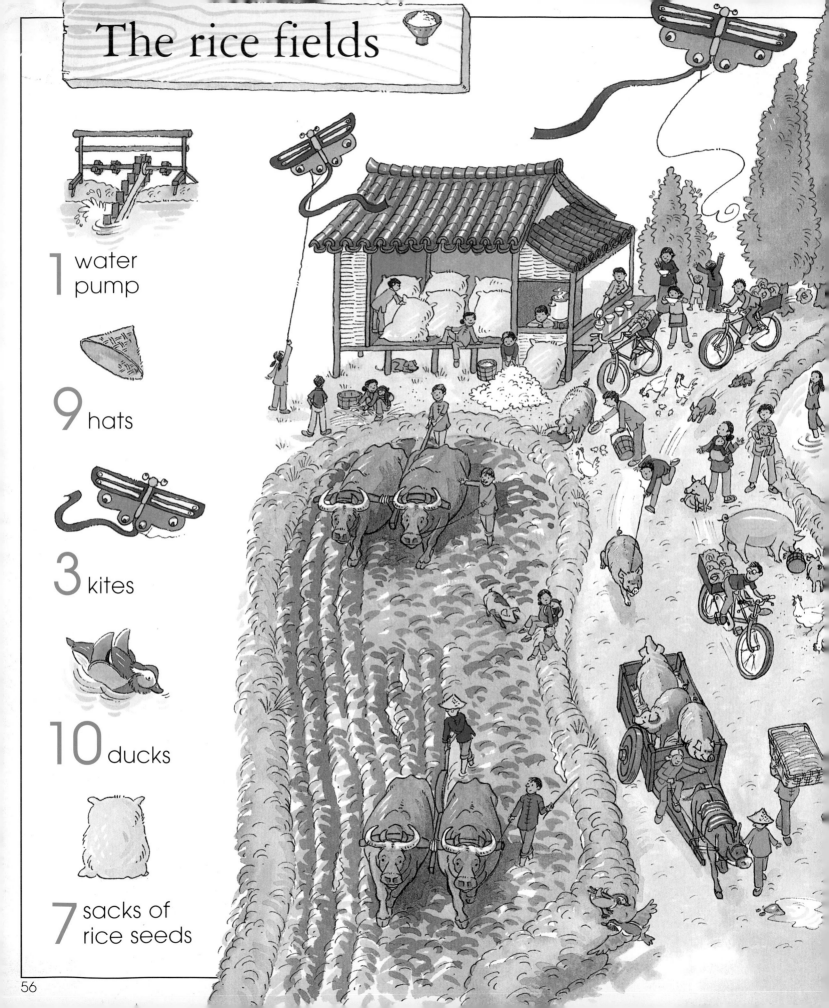

1 water pump

9 hats

3 kites

10 ducks

7 sacks of rice seeds

4 water buffaloes

 8 baskets of rice plants

 5 babies in slings

 3 bicycles

 5 black pigs

# On the pond

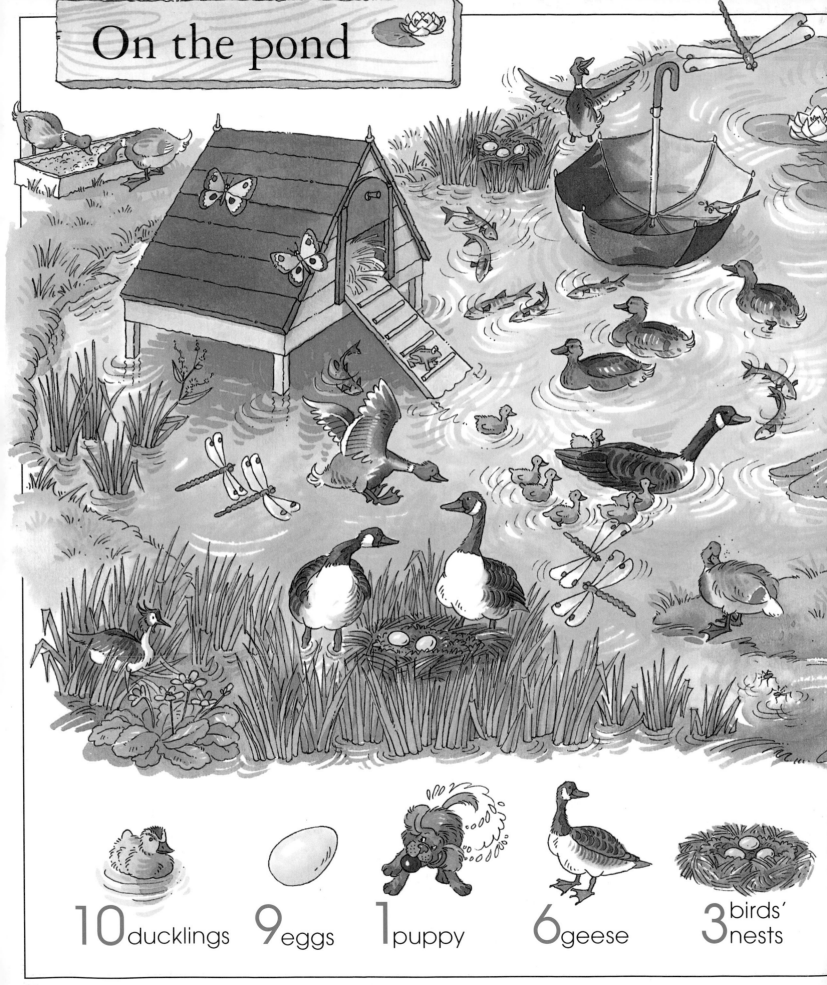

**10** ducklings  **9** eggs  **1** puppy  **6** geese  **3** birds' nests

58

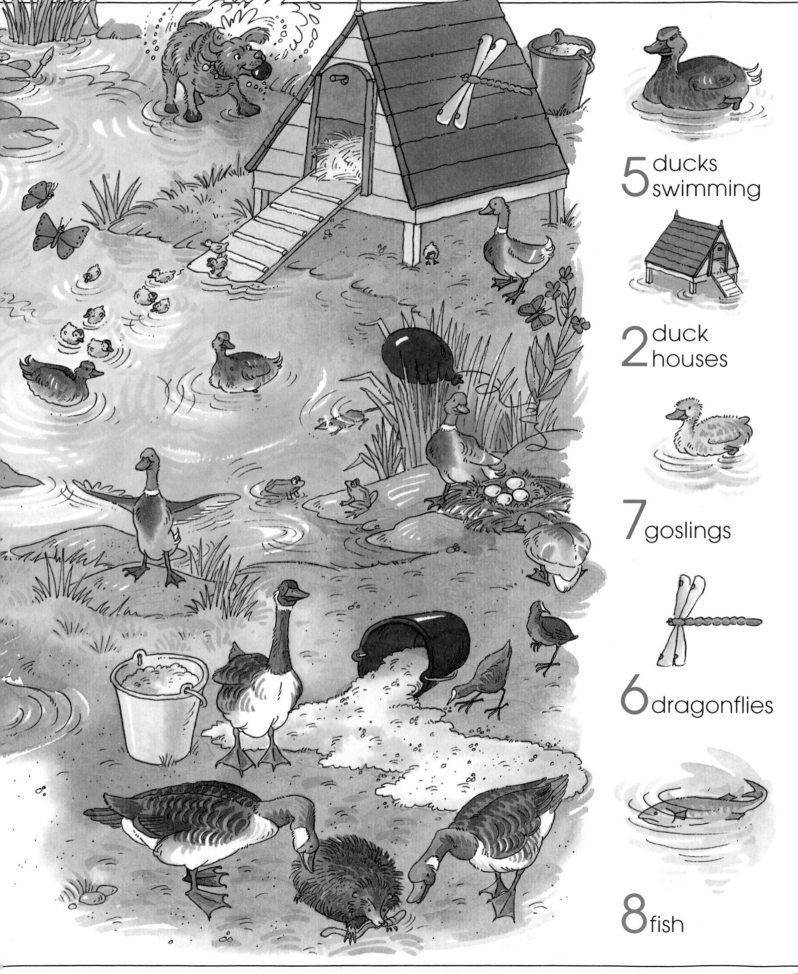

**5** ducks swimming

**2** duck houses

**7** goslings

**6** dragonflies

**8** fish

59

# On the ranch

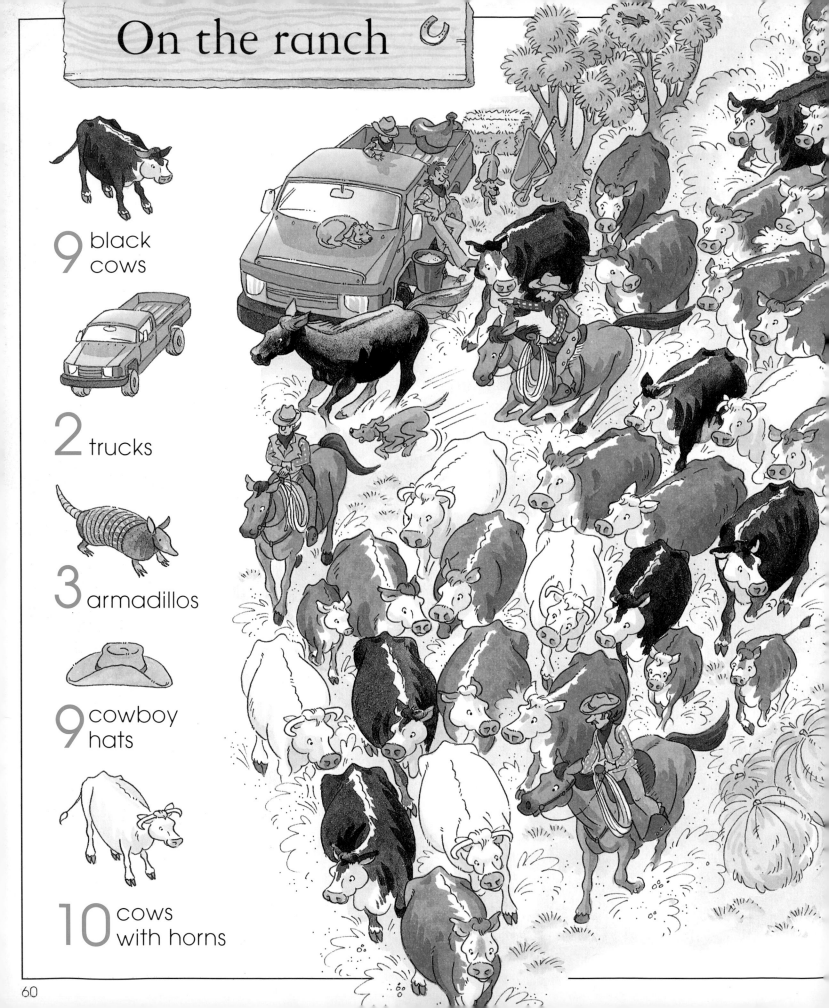

9 black cows

2 trucks

3 armadillos

9 cowboy hats

10 cows with horns

8 coils of rope  6 cowboys on horses  7 dogs  9 red bandanas  3 black horses

# The honey farm

5 box-shaped beehives

4 smoke machines

5 bars of honey soap

9 pots of honey

3 pairs of white gloves

**2** house-shaped beehives

**3** white suits

**7** dandelions

**6** beeswax candles

**1** pair of green boots

# Tropical farm

2 sloths

5 toucans

10 cocoa pods

7 monkeys

8 sacks of coffee beans

64

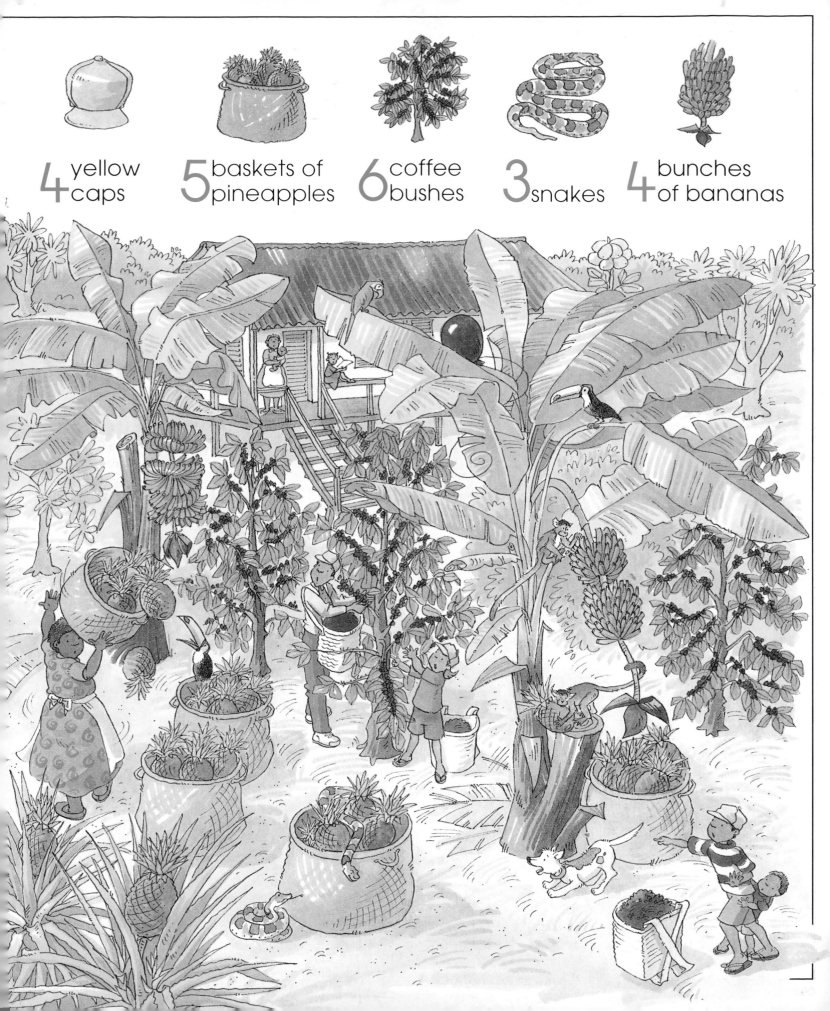

4 yellow caps

5 baskets of pineapples

6 coffee bushes

3 snakes

4 bunches of bananas

# The scarecrow

This scarecrow is made from things found on the farms in this section. Look back and see if you can find which page each thing is from.

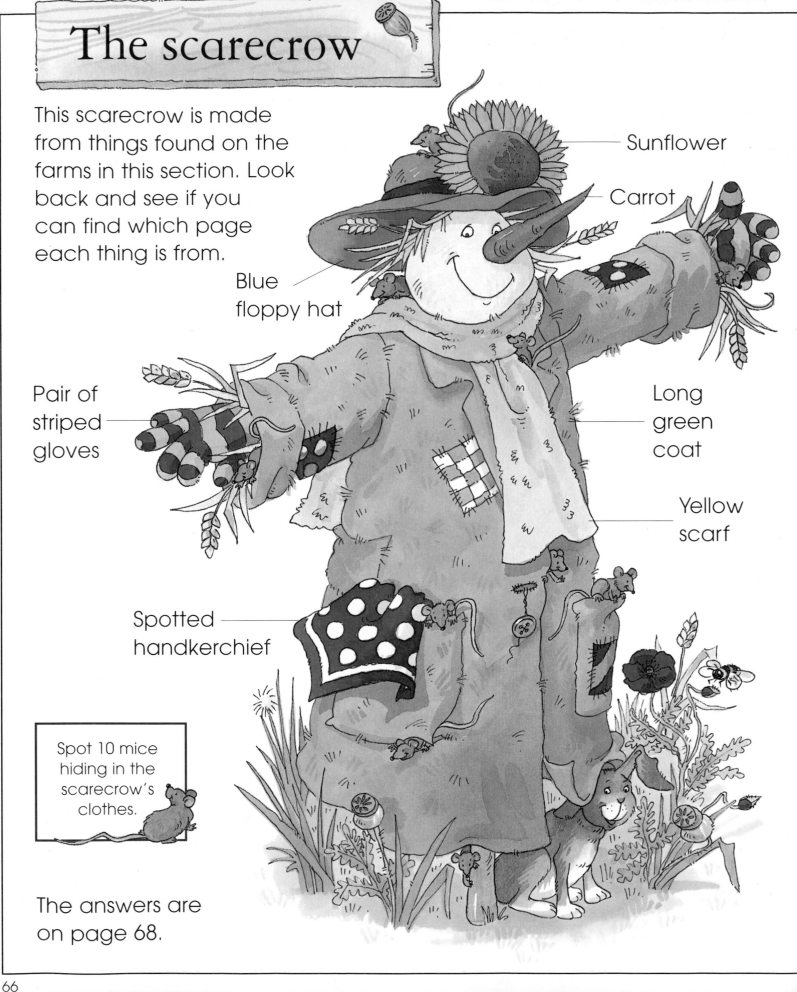

Sunflower

Carrot

Blue floppy hat

Pair of striped gloves

Long green coat

Yellow scarf

Spotted handkerchief

Spot 10 mice hiding in the scarecrow's clothes.

The answers are on page 68.

# More things to spot

Did you spot these things too? Look back and see if you can find them all.

4 moles

8 blue butterflies

2 rakes

9 yellow butterflies

2 umbrellas

8 blue buckets

6 wheelbarrows

7 yellow buckets

6 brooms

3 squirrels

4 shovels

9 frogs

How many people can you spot on each of the farms in this section? Some of them are small or partly hidden, so you will need to search very carefully. The answers are on page 68.

# Answers

## The scarecrow

The sunflower is on page 43 (The fruit farm).
The carrot is on page 44 (The greenhouse).
The blue floppy hat is on page 49 (Baby animals).
The striped gloves are on page 63 (The honey farm).
The long green coat is on page 40 (The sheep farm).
The yellow scarf is on page 47 (Milking time).
The spotted handkerchief is on page 54 (The henhouse).

## More things to spot

Did you manage to spot all the extra things too?
Here's where they all were:

**Moles**
The sheep farm: 2
Milking time: 1
Harvest time: 1

**Blue butterflies**
The greenhouse: 1
The henhouse: 1
On the pond: 3
The honey farm: 3

**Rakes**
Milking time: 1
Baby animals: 1

**Yellow butterflies**
The greenhouse: 2
The henhouse: 2
On the pond: 2
The honey farm: 3

**Umbrellas**
The rice fields: 1

On the pond: 1
**Blue buckets**
Milking time: 2
Baby animals: 1
Harvest time: 1
The henhouse: 1
On the pond: 1
On the ranch: 2

**Wheelbarrows**
The fruit farm: 1
Baby animals: 1
At the stables: 2
On the ranch: 2

**Yellow buckets**
Milking time: 3
At the stables: 3
On the pond: 1

**Brooms**
The sheep farm: 1

Milking time: 2
At the stables: 2
On the ranch: 1

**Squirrels**
Milking time : 1
At the stables: 1
The honey farm: 1

**Shovels**
Baby animals: 1
Harvest time: 1
At the stables: 2

**Frogs**
The greenhouse: 1
Milking time: 1
Baby animals: 2
The henhouse: 1
The rice fields: 1
On the pond: 3

Did you count the people on each farm? Here's how many there were:

The sheep farm: 11
The fruit farm: 32
The greenhouse: 0
Milking time: 10
Baby animals: 0

Harvest time: 22
At the stables: 21
The henhouse: 0
The rice fields: 69

On the pond: 0
On the ranch: 18
The honey farm: 3
Tropical farm: 12

## Acknowledgements

The publishers would like to thank the following individuals and organizations for providing information:

Agricultural advisor: Liza Dibble

Fullwood Ltd, Dairy Equipment Manufacturers, Shropshire, U.K.

Frances Wood, Curator of the Chinese Collections, British Library, London, U.K.

James Hamill, Beekeeping consultant, The Hive Honey Shop, London, U.K.

The Ranching Heritage Association, Texas, U.S.A.

Editor: Kamini Khanduri
Managing editor: Felicity Brooks
Managing designer: Mary Cartwright

# 1001
# Things to Spot
# in the Town

# Contents

# Things to spot

The pictures in this section show scenes from different towns around the world, including a bustling market, a busy fishing port and a river town. On every page there are lots of things for you to find and count.

This vibrant carnival scene is on pages 96–97.

Each little picture shows you what to look for in the big picture.

The blue number tells you how many of that thing you need to find.

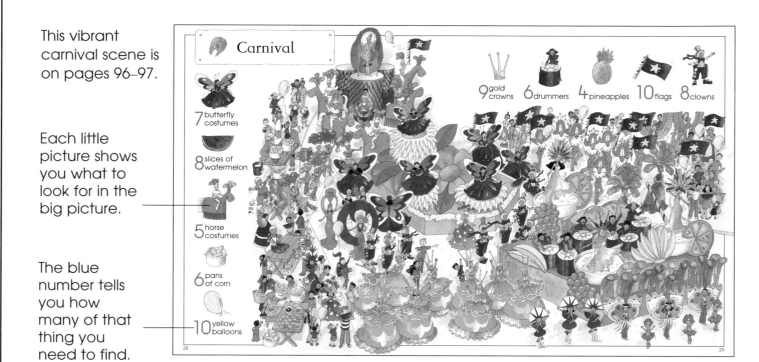

Carnival

7 butterfly costumes

8 slices of watermelon

5 horse costumes

6 pans of corn

10 yellow balloons

9 gold crowns    6 drummers    4 pineapples    10 flags    8 clowns

28

29

This is Sam. She visited each of the towns you'll see. Can you spot her in each scene?

Sam took photos of her trip and she brought things back from each town. On pages 98 and 99 you can look at these things and there are two puzzles for you to do.

# Street café

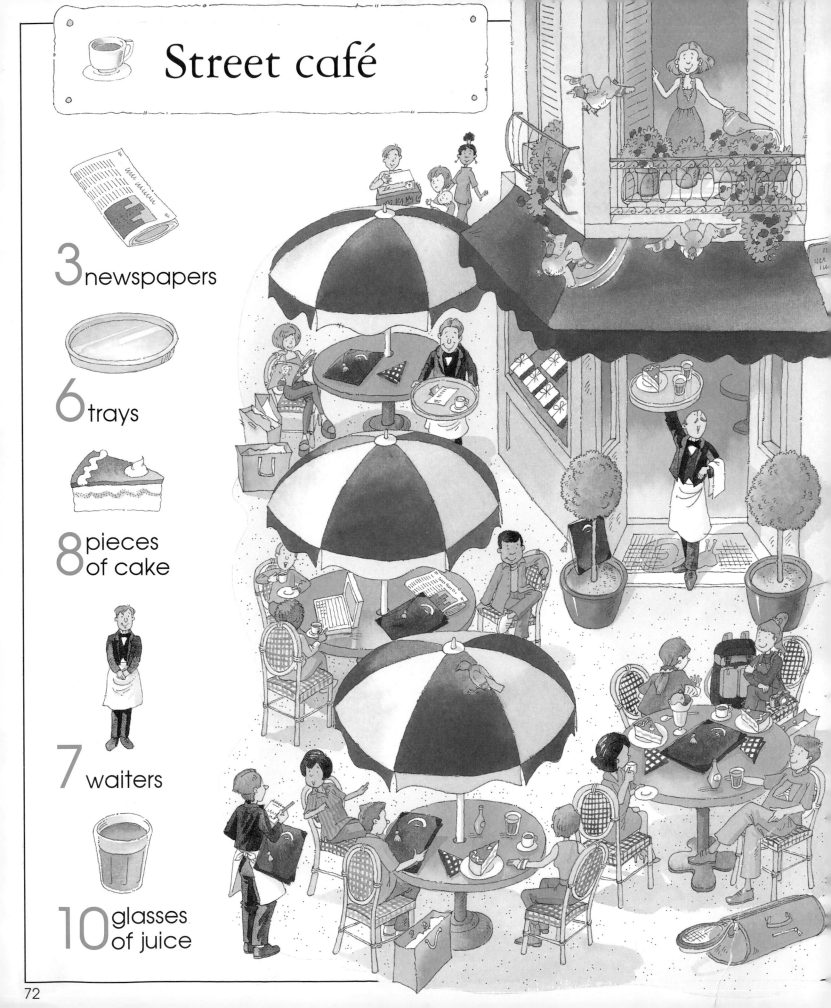

3 newspapers

6 trays

8 pieces of cake

7 waiters

10 glasses of juice

9 pigeons

6 parasols

5 ice creams

10 menus

1 musician

73

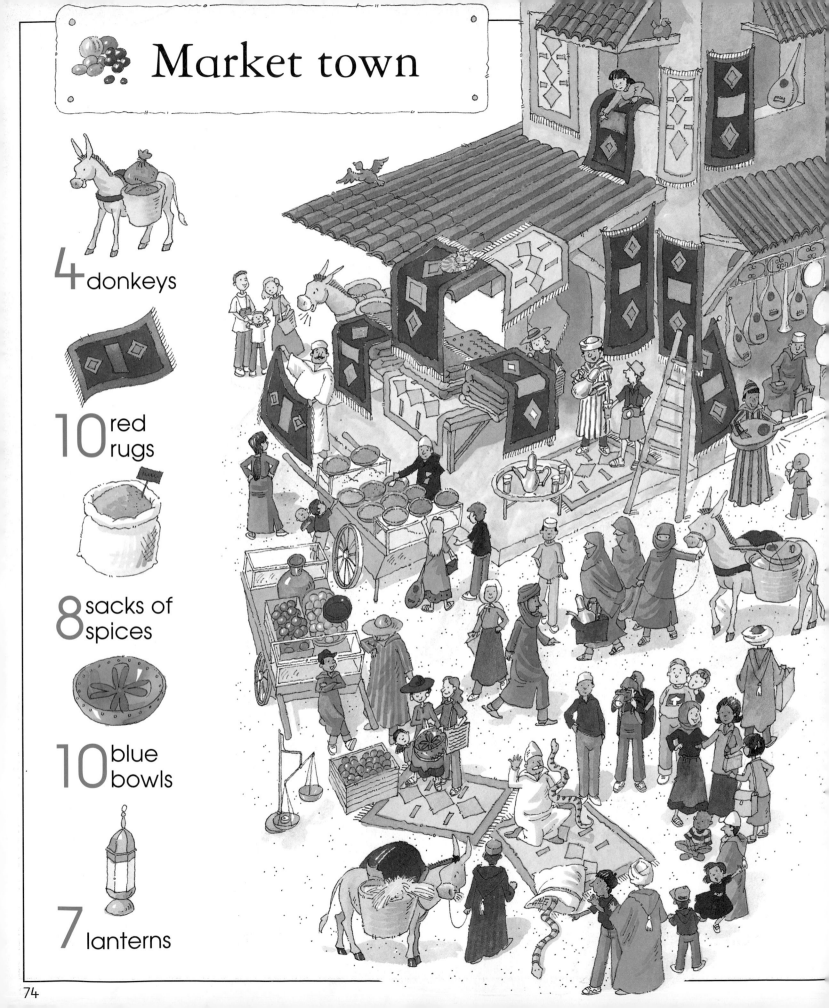

# Market town

4 donkeys

10 red rugs

8 sacks of spices

10 blue bowls

7 lanterns

74

**9** crates of oranges

**2** snakes

**3** carts

**7** teapots

**6** mirrors

# Nightlife

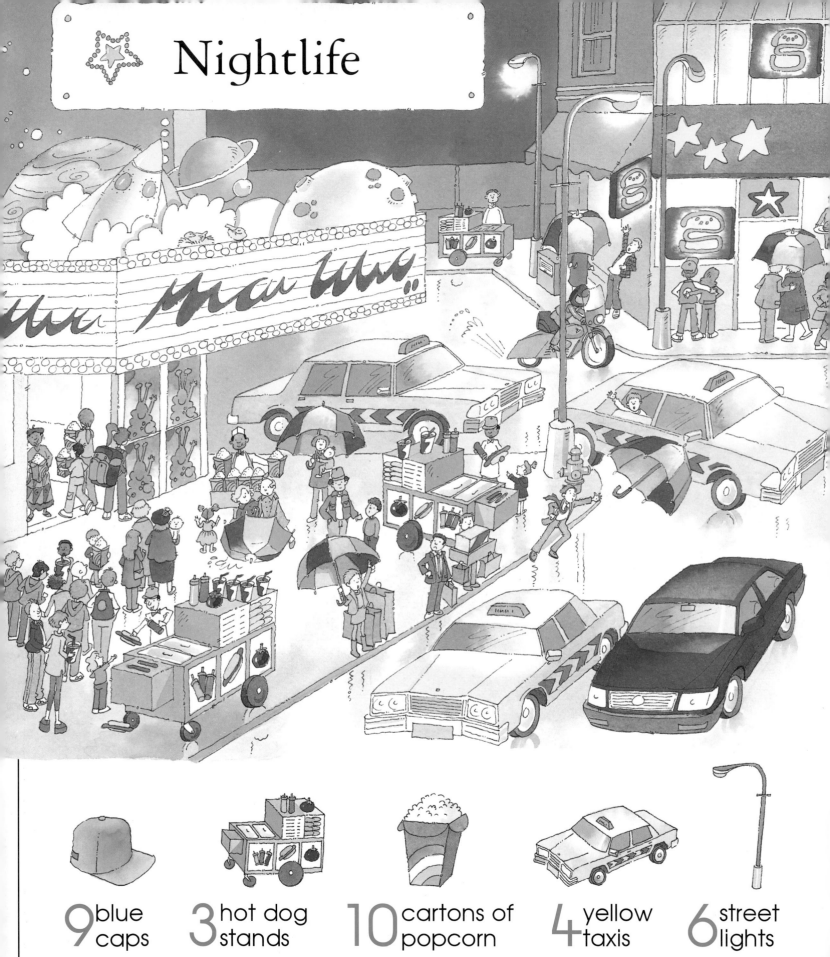

**9** blue caps

**3** hot dog stands

**10** cartons of popcorn

**4** yellow taxis

**6** street lights

1 ticket seller

 8 drinks with straws

 1 girl running

 3 burger signs

 10 umbrellas

# River town

8 baskets of bananas
7 washing lines
2 pots of red flowers
5 tubs of laundry
4 monks

1 ferry

10 straw hats

7 children splashing

6 baskets of rice

9 baskets of peppers

# Town square

1 fountain

7 pink arches

10 school bags

9 pigeons flying

4 street artists

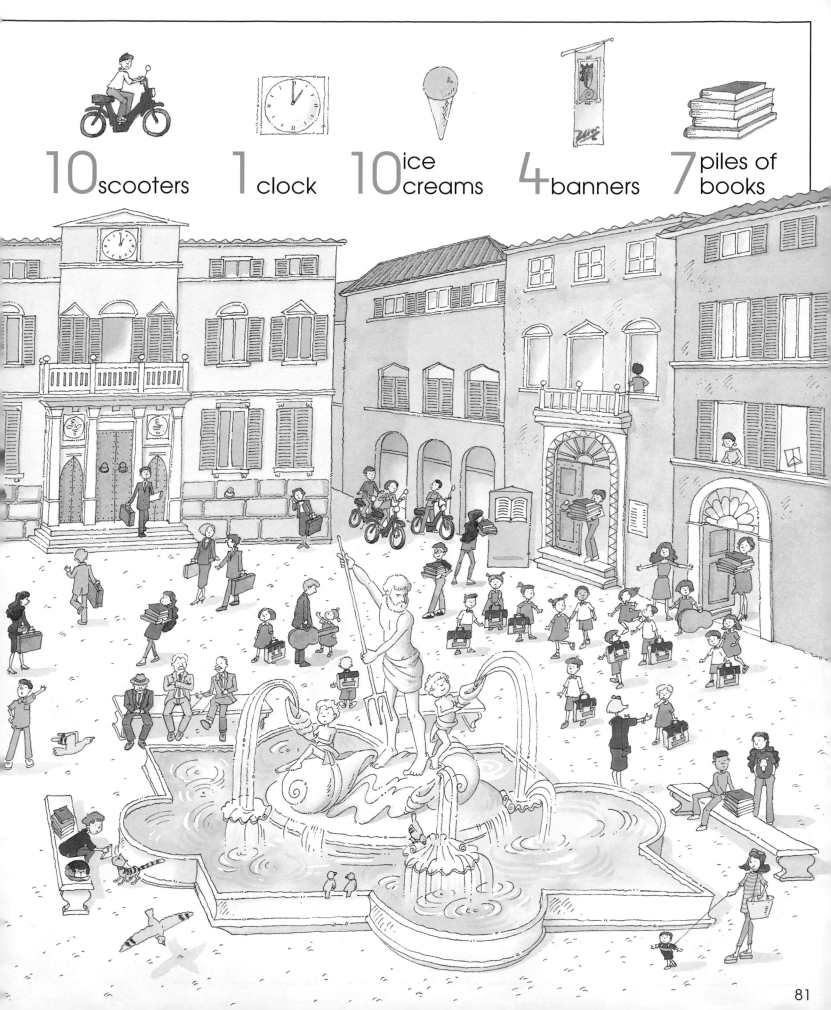

10 scooters  1 clock  10 ice creams  4 banners  7 piles of books

81

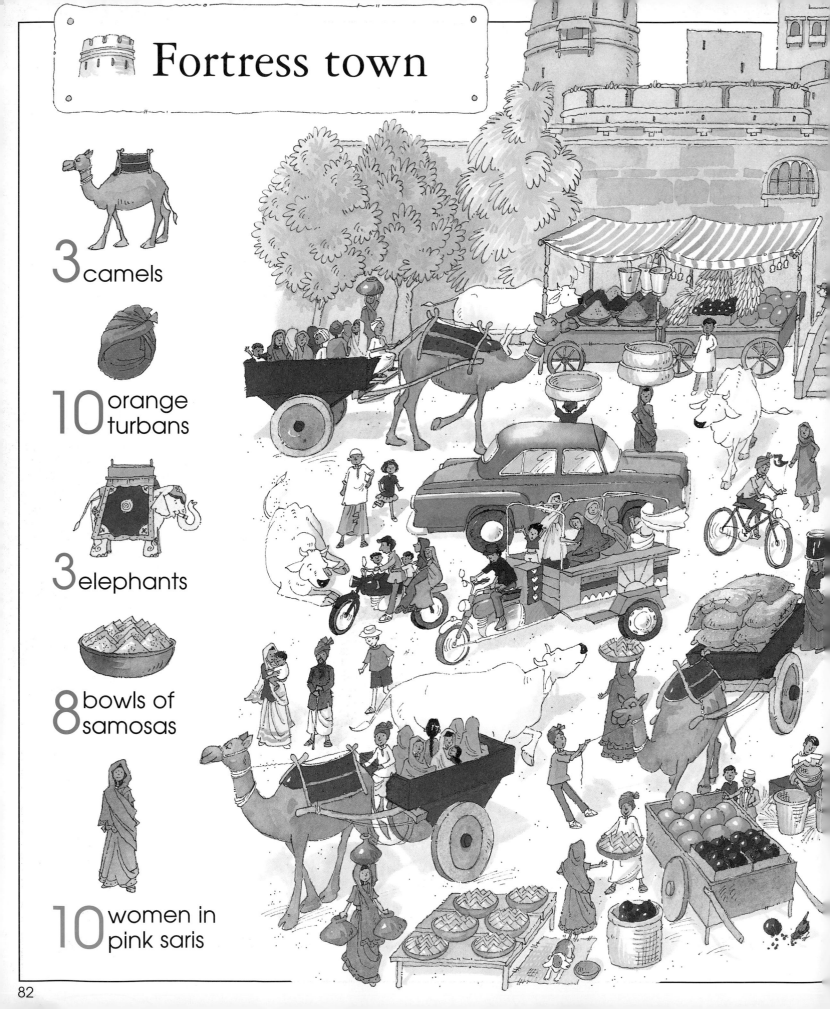

# Fortress town

**3** camels

**10** orange turbans

**3** elephants

**8** bowls of samosas

**10** women in pink saris

**10** sacks  **8** cows  **9** flower garlands  **1** gateway  **10** blue books

# Town park

2 kites

3 swings

9 ducklings

8 soccer players

2 red boats

10 red tulips

8 dogs

5 benches

8 squirrels

84

6 people
skating

# Traffic jam

**8** green taxis

**2** road signs

**10** bicycles

**3** buses

**9** brown briefcases

**10** school boys

**2** trucks

**8** blue cars

**1** street barber

**2** bus stops

87

# Fishing port

8 cats

5 empty buckets

10 seagulls

7 crab pots

3 nets

9 crabs　　10 buckets of fish　　6 fishermen　　2 postcard stands　　4 boats

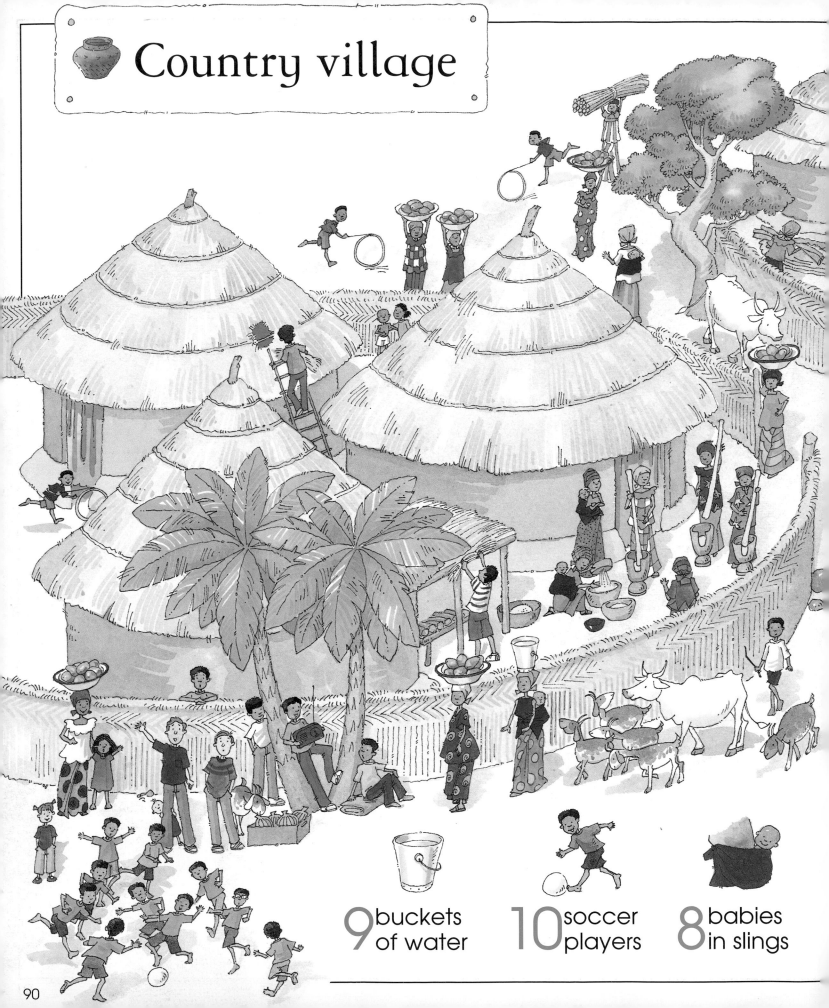

# Country village

9 buckets of water

10 soccer players

8 babies in slings

9 women pounding grain

4 children with hoops

9 dishes of mangoes

1 well

10 goats

7 huts

9 striped headscarves

# Shopping street

 9 skateboards

 7 shoeboxes

 8 striped T-shirts

10 beach balls

 6 swimsuits

**9** toy kangaroos    **6** jars of lollipops    **8** flowery dresses    **10** red bags    **8** kookaburras

# Snowy town

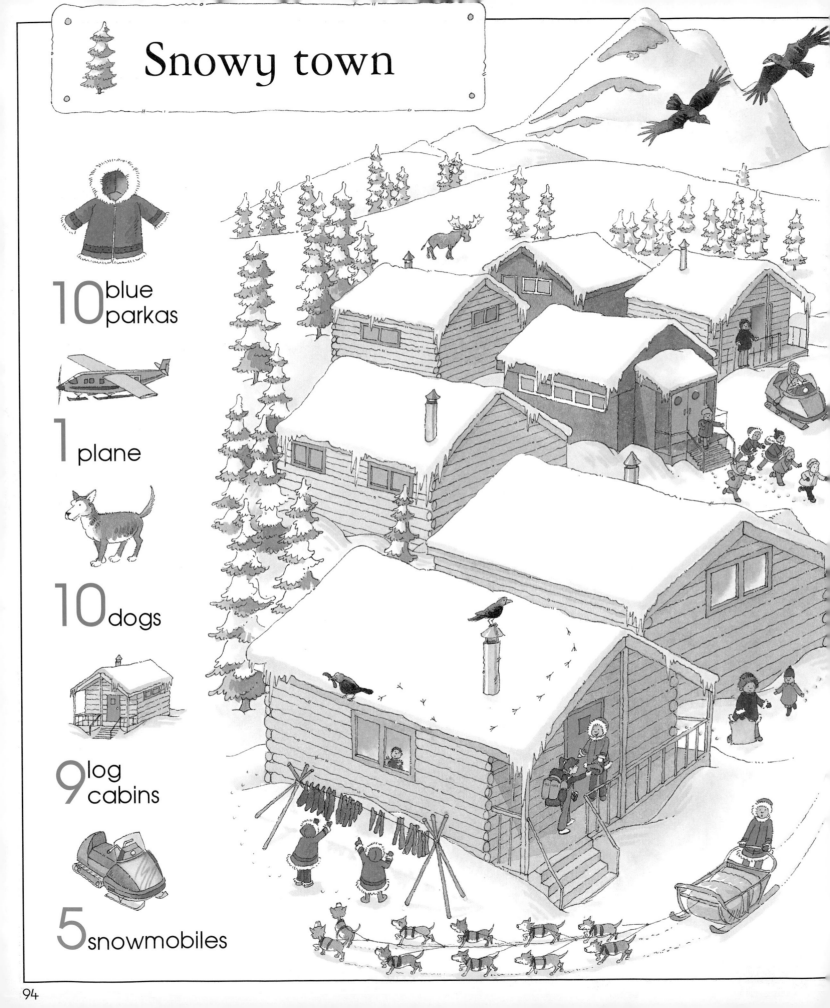

10 blue parkas

1 plane

10 dogs

9 log cabins

5 snowmobiles

94

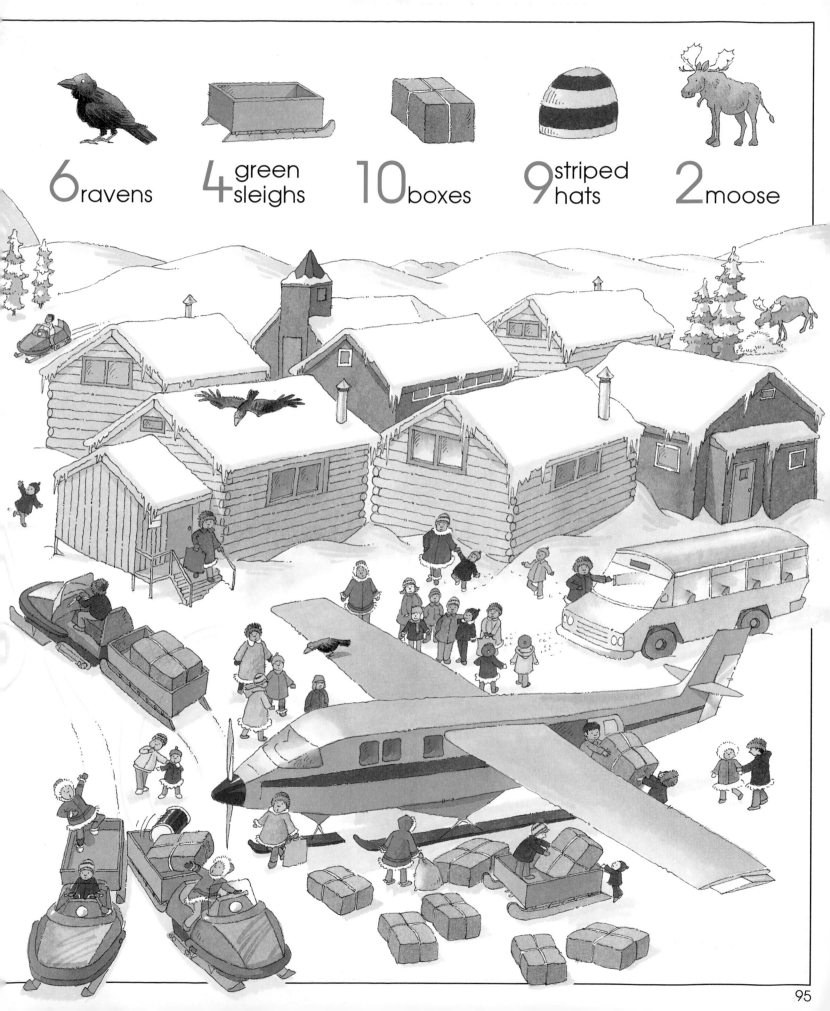

6 ravens

4 green sleighs

10 boxes

9 striped hats

2 moose

# Carnival

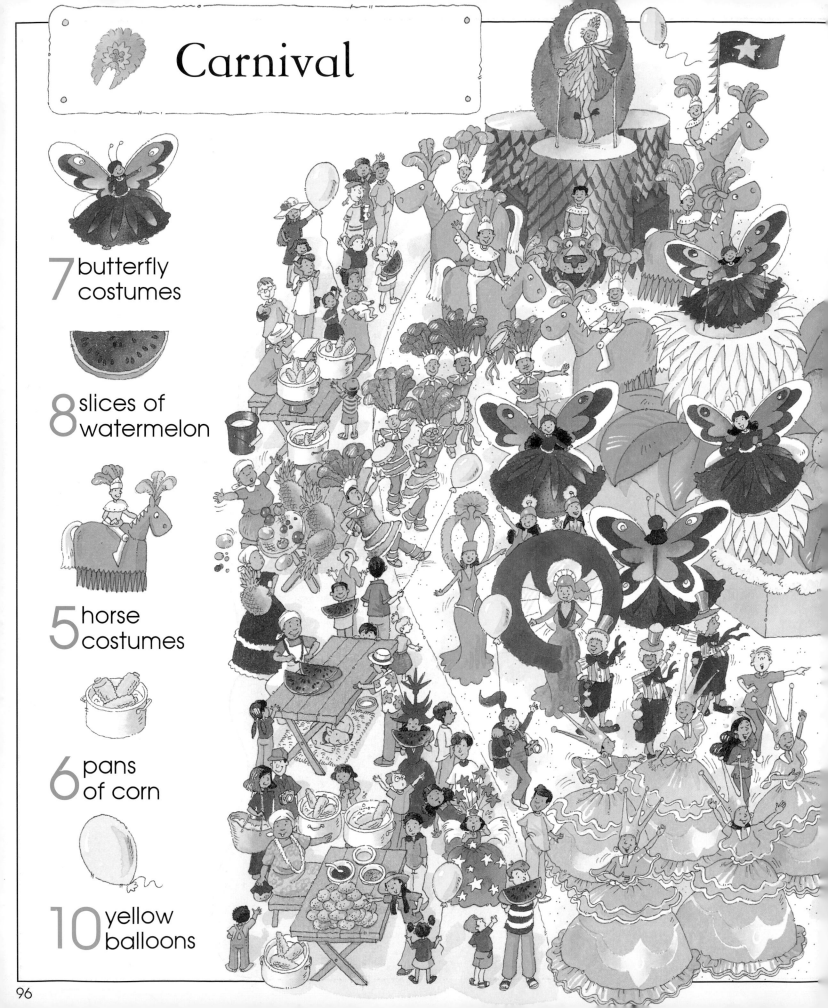

**7** butterfly costumes

**8** slices of watermelon

**5** horse costumes

**6** pans of corn

**10** yellow balloons

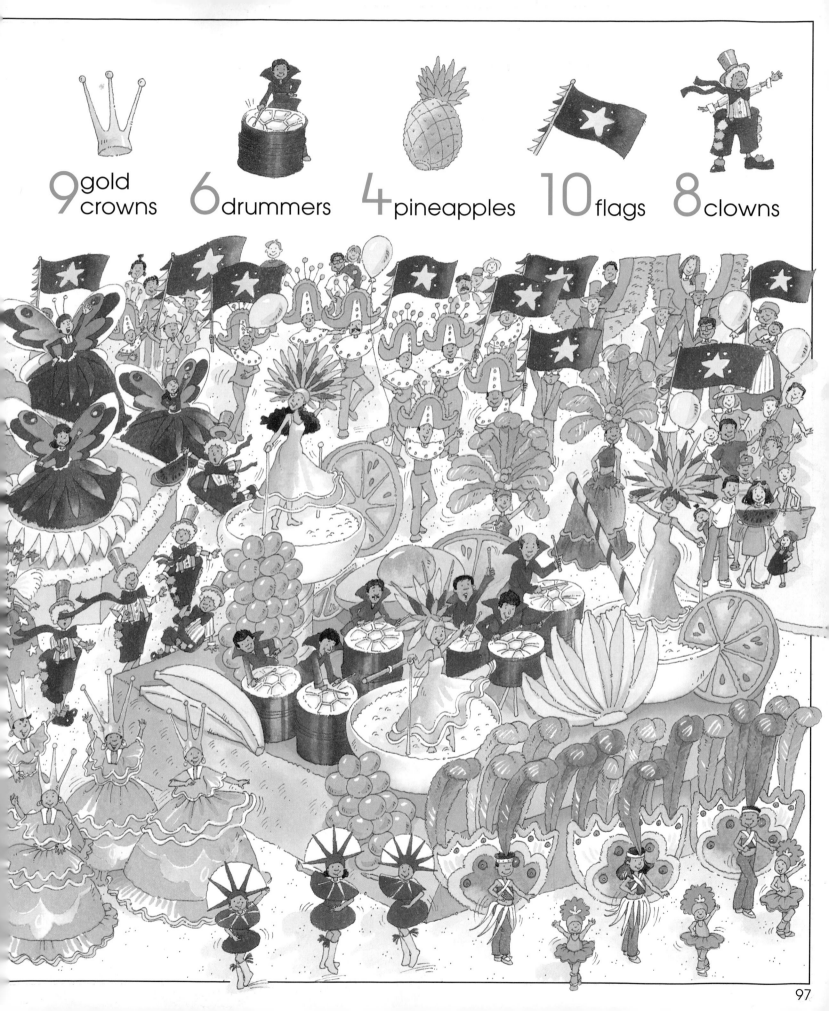

**9** gold crowns  **6** drummers  **4** pineapples  **10** flags  **8** clowns

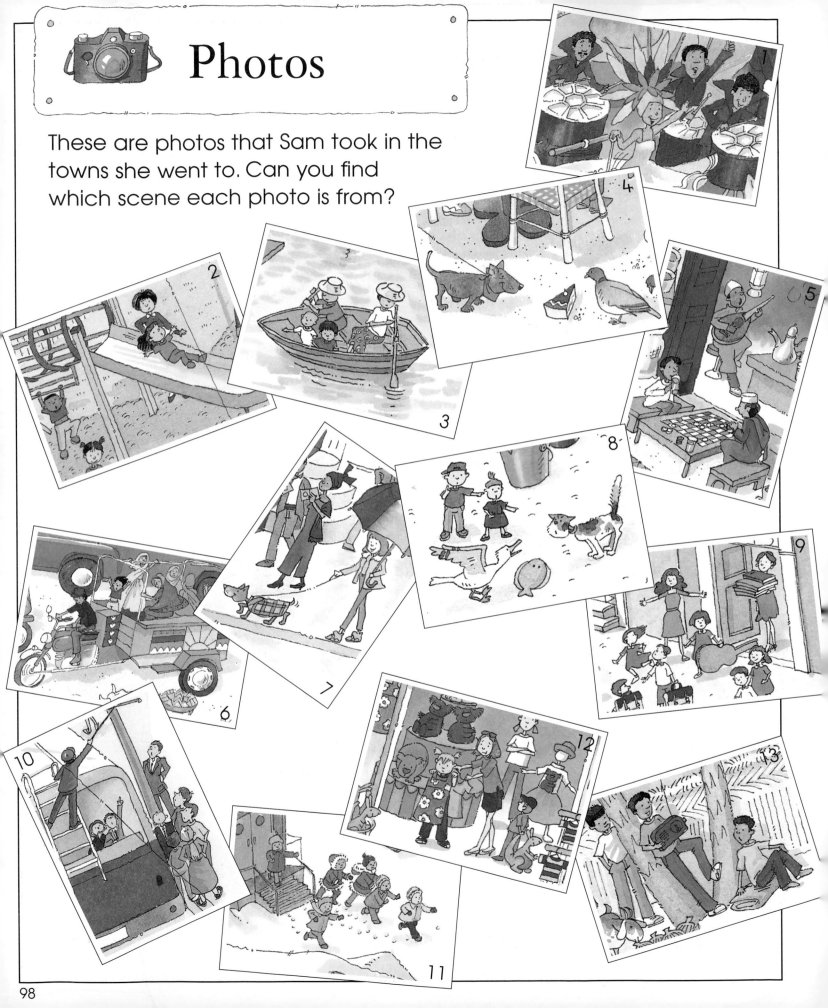

# Photos

These are photos that Sam took in the towns she went to. Can you find which scene each photo is from?

# Souvenirs

Sam brought these souvenirs back from the towns she visited. Can you find which towns they are from and count them all?

10 blue and white teapots

10 striped bags

4 posters of aliens

10 yellow shells

9 wooden elephants

8 orange feathers

10 brown fur hats

7 starfish

4 boxes of chocolates

9 yellow rugs

5 cake boxes

10 balloons with faces

3 koras

9 napkins

2 paper boats

9 puppets

# Answers

Did you find all the photos and souvenirs? Here's where they are.

## Photos

1 Carnival
(page 97)

2 Town park
(page 85)

3 River town
(page 78)

4 Street café
(page 73)

5 Market town
(page 75)

6 Fortress town
(page 82)

7 Nightlife
(page 77)

8 Fishing port
(page 89)

9 Town square
(page 81)

10 Traffic jam
(page 87)

11 Snowy town
(page 94)

12 Shopping street
(page 92)

13 Country village
(page 90)

## Souvenirs

10 blue and white teapots:
Traffic jam
(pages 86 and 87)

10 striped bags:
Shopping street
(pages 92 and 93)

4 posters of aliens:
Nightlife
(pages 76 and 77)

10 yellow shells:
Fishing port
(pages 88 and 89)

9 wooden elephants:
River town
(pages 78 and 79)

8 orange feathers:
Carnival
(pages 96 and 97)

10 brown fur hats:
Snowy town
(pages 94 and 95)

7 starfish:
Fishing port
(pages 88 and 89)

4 boxes of chocolates:
Street café
(pages 72 and 73)

9 yellow rugs:
Market town
(pages 74 and 75)

5 cake boxes:
Street café
(pages 72 and 73)

10 balloons with faces:
Town square
(pages 80 and 81)

3 koras:
Country village
(pages 90 and 91)

9 napkins:
Street café
(pages 72 and 73)

2 paper boats:
Town park
(pages 84 and 85)

9 puppets:
Fortress town
(pages 82 and 83)

## Acknowledgements

Editor: Gillian Doherty
Managing editor: Felicity Brooks
Managing designer: Mary Cartwright
Additional design: Nicola Butler

The publishers would also like to thank the following people for providing information about different towns:

Caroline Liou, China
Cheryl Ward, Australia
Daryl Bowers, Barrow, Alaska
Mr Jensen, Dan Fishing Equipment Ltd., Denmark
Frances Linzee Gordon, Morocco
Helene Kratzsch and Marie Rose von Wesendonk
Ibrahim Keith Holt, The Council of

the Obsidian, West Africa Office
Imogen Franks, Lonely Planet Publications
Michael Willis, Curator, British Museum
Susannah Selwyn, ES International Language Schools

# 1001
# Things to Spot
# Long Ago

# Contents

# Things to spot

The pictures in this section show scenes from long ago. You can see a Viking ship, visit an Egyptian pharaoh's court and explore a busy market from 4,000 years ago. On every page there are lots of things for you to find and count.

This tells you when and where the scene took place. You can see this castle feast on pages 114–115.

Each little picture shows you what to look for in the big picture.

The blue number shows how many of that thing you need to find.

A castle feast
England, 600 years ago

2 roasted peacocks   3 trumpets   1 juggler   8 jugs   7 pies   10 knives   2 lutes   10 silver goblets   5 fish   6 money pouches

There are lots of other things to spot scattered throughout this section of the book. You can find out what you need to do to find them on pages 130 and 131.

There's a spider like this one hidden in each big picture. Can you find them all?

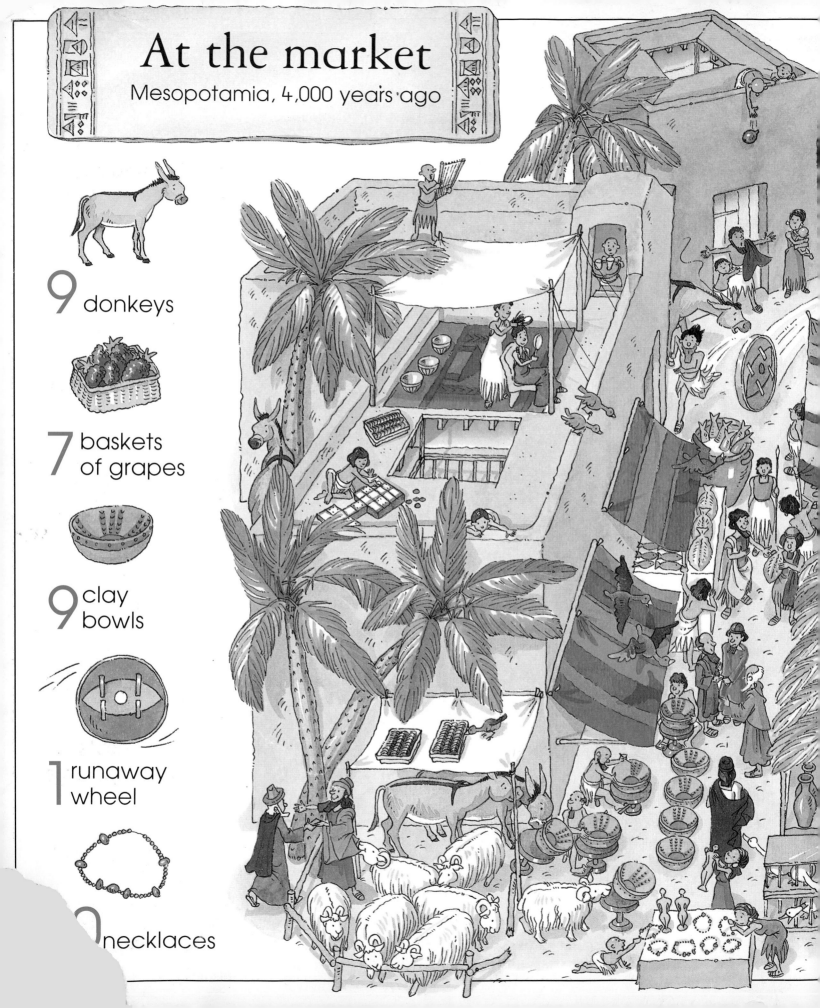

# At the market
## Mesopotamia, 4,000 years ago

9 donkeys

7 baskets of grapes

9 clay bowls

1 runaway wheel

9 necklaces

**9** baskets of dates

**10** sacks of grain

**8** palm trees

**6** baskets of apricots

**10** copper bowls

105

# Pharaoh's court
## Egypt, 3,500 years ago

10 beaded collars

9 white fans

2 pairs of red sandals

3 stools

10 wine jars

4 monkeys    1 harp    3 patterned rugs    10 bracelets    2 chests

# Watching a play
### Greece, 2,300 years ago

1 mask with a beard

9 red cushions

1 crane

10 people laughing

**8** people eating

**1** man sleeping   **8** hats   **1** lyre   **4** green tunics   **1** altar

# In the garden

Rome, 2,000 years ago

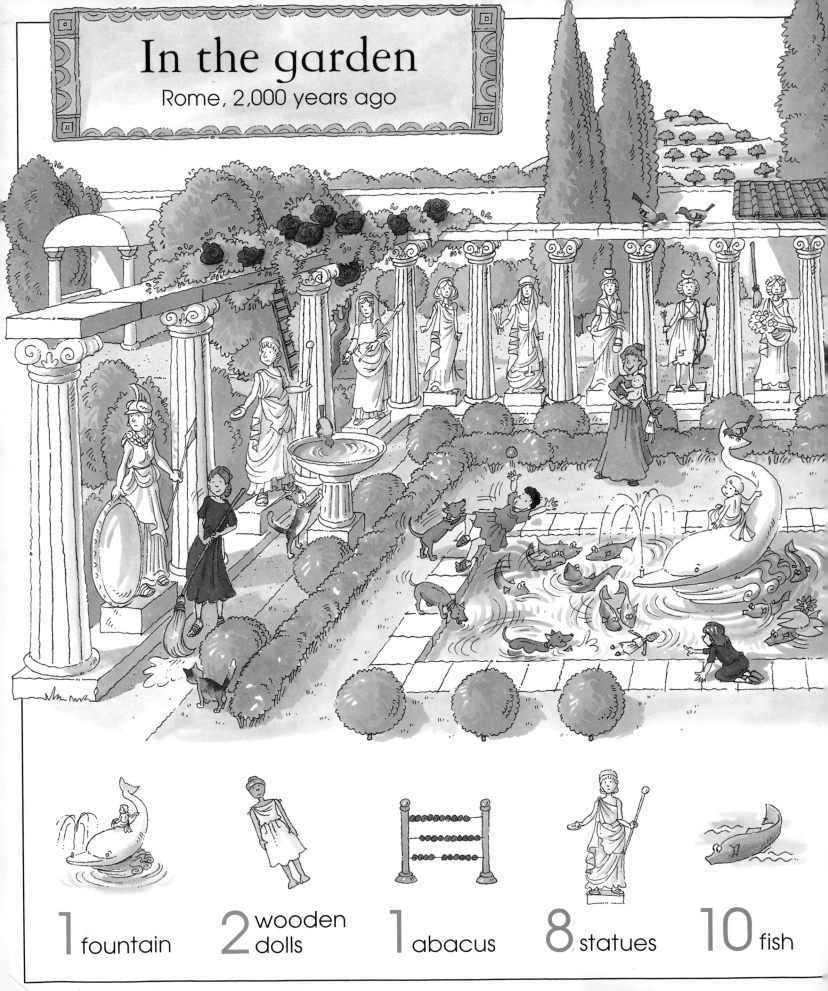

1 fountain

2 wooden dolls

1 abacus

8 statues

10 fish

**10** red roses   **3** scrolls   **9** birds   **2** slaves sweeping   **10** apples

# A Viking voyage

Norway, 1,200 years ago

10 seagulls

9 chests

5 red cloaks

2 wagons

8 headscarves

**10** plain shields  **6** sheep  **10** barrels  **8** axes  **9** chickens

# A castle feast
England, 600 years ago

**2** roasted peacocks   **3** trumpets   **1** juggler   **8** jugs   **7** pies

10 knives  2 lutes  10 silver goblets  5 fish  6 money pouches

# The artists' workshop
## Italy, 550 years ago

8 paint palettes

7 mallets

8 sketches

9 writing quills

10 paintbrushes

6 dirty shirts

7 easels

1 portrait of a lady

5 pots of red paint

6 black rats

# An Inca farm
## Peru, 500 years ago

**9** hoes

**8** babies in slings

**5** people scaring birds

**10** baskets of corn

118

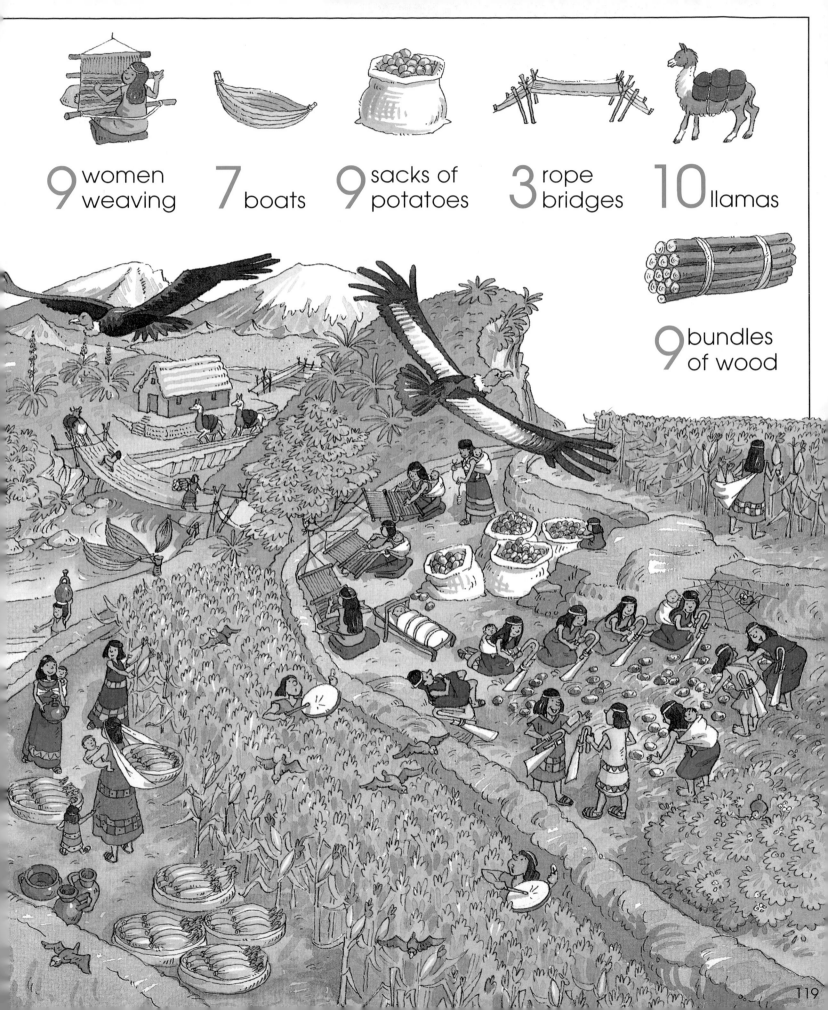

9 women weaving

7 boats

9 sacks of potatoes

3 rope bridges

10 llamas

9 bundles of wood

119

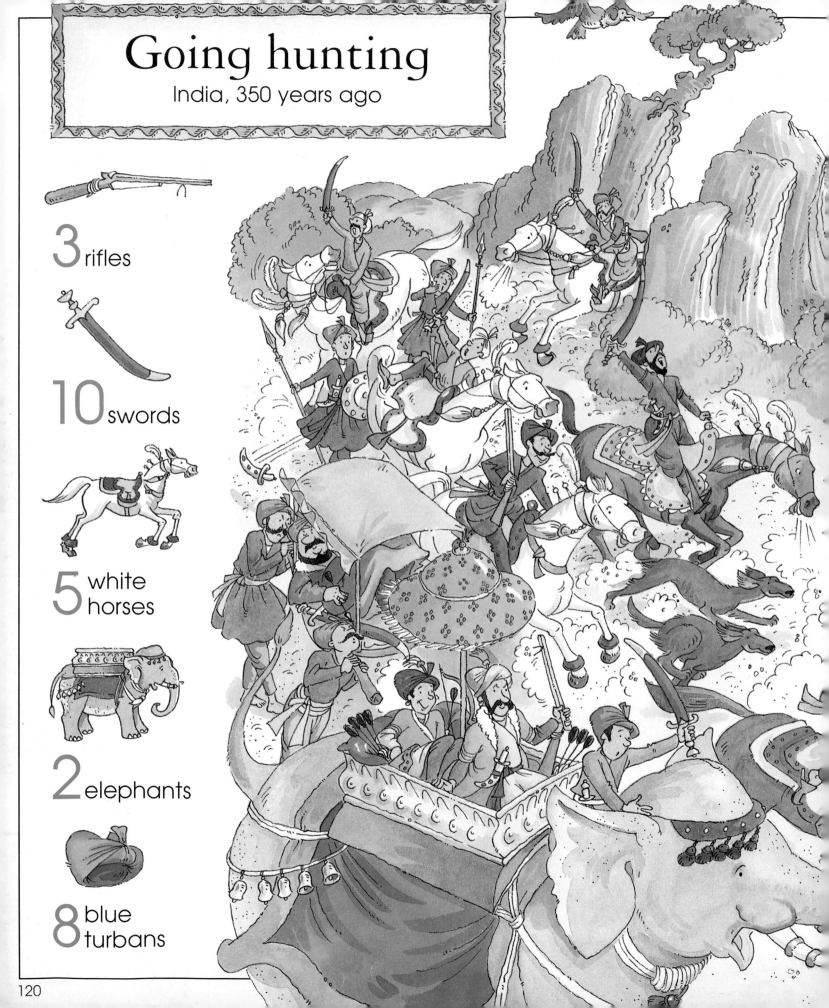

# Going hunting
### India, 350 years ago

3 rifles

10 swords

5 white horses

2 elephants

8 blue turbans

3 tigers

10 gold tassels

9 arrows

6 hunting dogs

9 white feathers

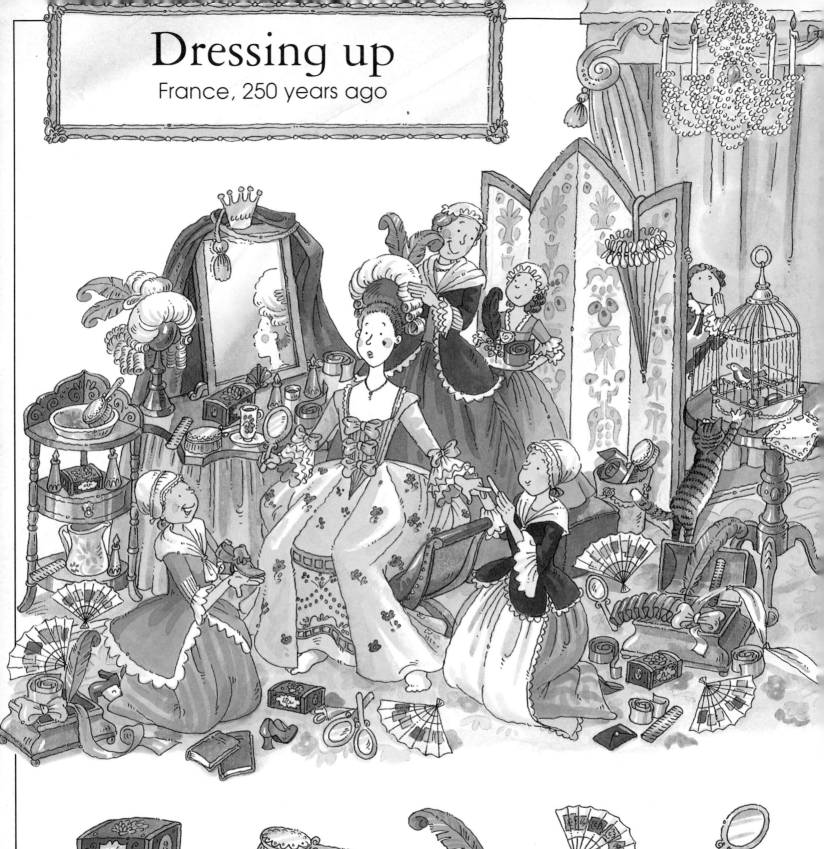

# Dressing up
## France, 250 years ago

 **7** decorated boxes

 **5** hairbrushes

 **9** blue feathers

 **8** fans

 **4** hand mirrors

1 bird in a cage

6 pink ribbons

3 cats

2 parasols

10 yellow bows

# A wagon train
## North America, 200 years ago

**9** water bottles

**5** aprons

**10** oxen with white faces

**9** whips

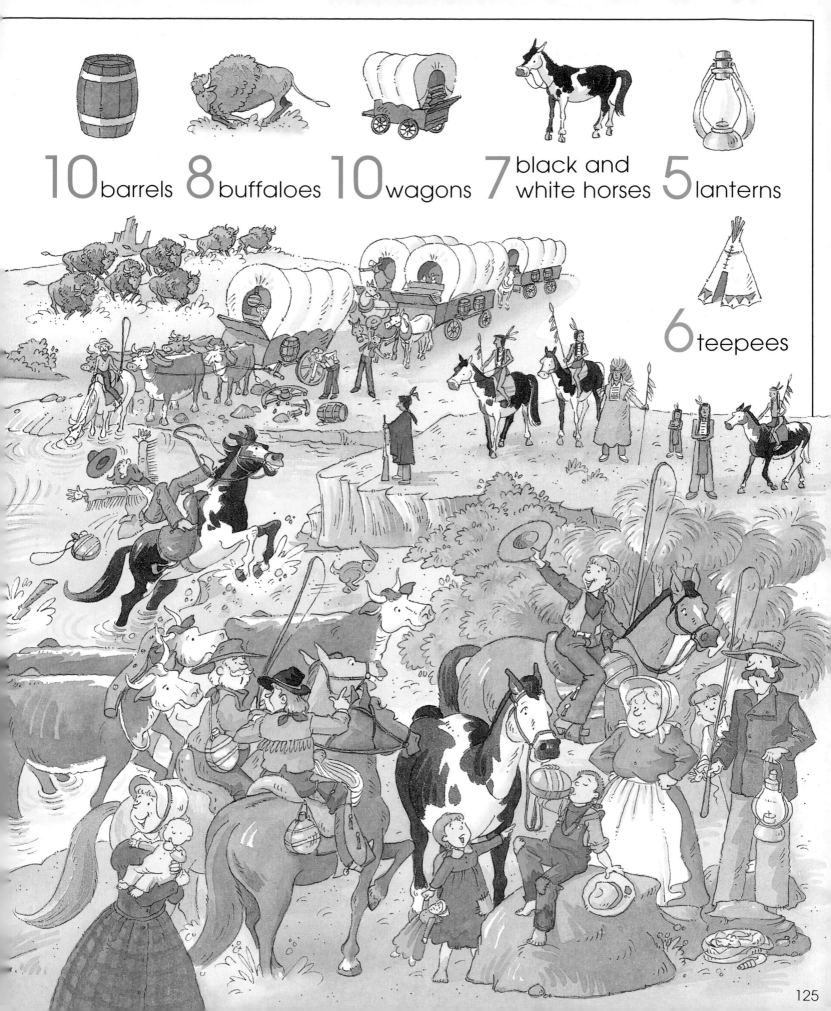

10 barrels  8 buffaloes  10 wagons  7 black and white horses  5 lanterns

6 teepees

125

# Going shopping
## England, 130 years ago

4 bells

7 dolls

3 rolls of red cloth

1 monkey

10 pigeons

5 baskets of flowers

1 rocking horse

4 lampposts

9 jars of sweets    8 shawls

# The drive-in movies

North America, 45 years ago

8 ketchup containers

9 drinks with straws

10 slices of pizza

9 boxes of popcorn

10 hot dogs

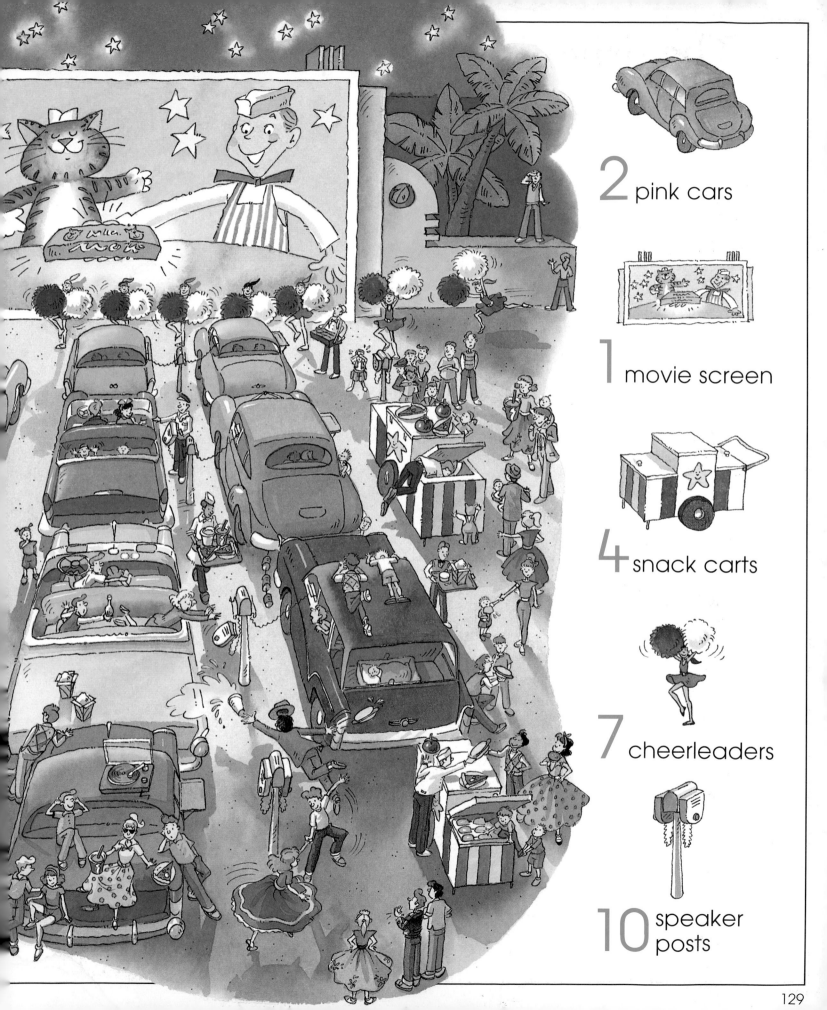

2 pink cars

1 movie screen

4 snack carts

7 cheerleaders

10 speaker posts

# At the museum

Museums help you to find out about life long ago. This museum contains things from this section of the book. Can you find which scene each thing is from? The answers are on page 132.

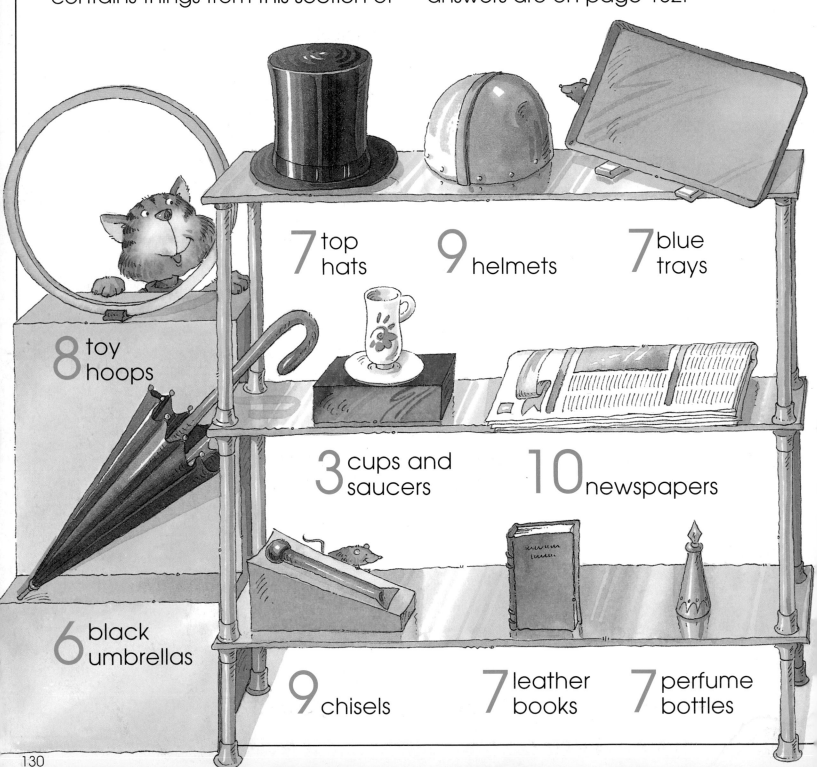

7 top hats

9 helmets

7 blue trays

8 toy hoops

3 cups and saucers

10 newspapers

6 black umbrellas

9 chisels

7 leather books

7 perfume bottles

6 cauldrons

3 cradles

7 red pompoms

10 silver spoons

8 flower pots

1 tailor's dummy

9 drinking horns

2 gold goblets

9 gold coins

9 blue cushions

8 keys

7 white pompoms

5 brooms

131

# Answers

Did you find all the things from the museum on pages 130 and 131? Here's where they are:

**8 toy hoops:**
Going shopping
(pages 126 and 127)

**6 black umbrellas:**
Going shopping
(pages 126 and 127)

**7 top hats:**
Going shopping
(pages 126 and 127)

**9 helmets:**
A Viking voyage
(pages 112 and 113)

**7 blue trays:**
The drive-in movies
(pages 128 and 129)

**3 cups and saucers:**
Dressing up
(pages 122 and 123)

**10 newspapers:**
Going shopping
(pages 126 and 127)

**9 chisels:**
The artists' workshop
(pages 116 and 117)

**7 leather books:**
Dressing up
(pages 122 and 123)

**7 perfume bottles:**
Dressing up
(pages 122 and 123)

**6 cauldrons:**
A Viking voyage
(pages 112 and 113)

**3 cradles:**
An Inca farm
(pages 118 and 119)

**7 red pompoms:**
The drive-in movies
(pages 128 and 129)

**10 silver spoons:**
A castle feast
(pages 114 and 115)

**8 flower pots:**
Going shopping
(pages 126 and 127)

**9 drinking horns:**
A Viking voyage
(pages 112 and 113)

**2 gold goblets:**
A castle feast
(pages 114 and 115)

**9 gold coins:**
A castle feast
(pages 114 and 115)

**9 blue cushions:**
Watching a play
(pages 108 and 109)

**8 keys:**
A castle feast
(pages 114 and 115)

**7 white pompoms:**
The drive-in movies
(pages 128 and 129)

**1 tailor's dummy:**
Going shopping
(pages 126 and 127)

**5 brooms:**
In the garden
(pages 110 and 111)

## Acknowledgements

Managing editor: Felicity Brooks   Managing designer: Mary Cartwright
History consultant: Anne Millard
With thanks to Don and Susan Sanders for advice on *The Drive-in movies*